DESMOND ELLIS was born in Dublin in 1944, and at four years of age started school in Gavan Duffy's, Earlsfort Terrace; from there, at the age of seven, he went to the Christian Brothers on Synge Street. Later he went to Mount Street Technical School, studied commercial art at night in Rathmines College and joined the Abbey Theatre School of Acting. In 1972, he set off for Canada, where he briefly worked as a paste-up artist for a school-book publisher, before taking up acting; he has been an actor in Canada ever since. His children's book, *The Undergardeners*, was recently published in Canada.

DESMOND ELLIS

Bockety

A MEMOIR

with illustrations by the author

A Brandon Original Paperback

First published in 2006 by
Brandon
an imprint of Mount Eagle Publications
Unit 3 Olympia Trading Estate, Coburg Road, London N22 6TZ, England
and Cooleen, Dingle, Co. Kerry, Ireland

www.brandonbooks.com

10 9 8 7 6 5 4 3 2 1

ISBN 0 86322 364 8

Cover design: Anú Design [www.anu-design.ie]
Cover photograph: Magnum Photos
Typesetting by Red Barn Publishing, Skeagh, Skibbereen
Printed in the UK

DEDICATION

This book is dedicated to the memory of my parents,
Chrissie and Seamus. Where it all began.

ACKNOWLEDGEMENTS

I am enormously grateful to my brother, Brendan, for all the
help he gave me with the book. His contribution cannot be
overestimated. Along with Brendan, Patricia and Noel are
also cherished for being part of the past where the
memories upon which this story is based reside. And thanks
to their spouses, John, Mary and Honor, for helping to keep
the memories growing.

Also dear to me is my aunt, Sheila Brennan, who was there from
the beginning and is still a friend; and to Lois MacLeod, another
friend, I also express my gratitude.

I am most grateful to Steve MacDonogh at
Brandon/Mount Eagle for having the courage of my convictions
and the confidence to publish *Bockety*.

And to Karen who read it first.

1

I DON'T KNOW why I was so amazed that Ronnie's nose spurted blood; after all, I'd just punched it. I supposed it was just myself I was amazed at for doing such a thing. I don't know what came over me. All Ronnie had done was ask me did I know how people could tell if you were a boy or a girl. I thought he'd gone a bit soft in the head. "Look," I said, pointing around the schoolyard. "There's the girls on that side. And there's the boys over there. How could you mix them up?"

"Yeah," he said. "But supposing I was blind? Explain it to me." What was he on about? It was obvious, wasn't it? Apart from anything else, the girls were the ones the boys weren't playing with.

"Well, for one thing, the girls . . ." I stopped. I tried again. "The boys are . . ." I felt stupid. Of course, I knew what the difference was, but I couldn't explain it: just to say that girls were the ones you didn't want to play with didn't seem to be a good enough answer.

"How do you mean?" I asked, playing for time.

Ronnie pointed down below his waist and said, "That's the difference."

I looked down and then looked around the schoolyard. Of course! "The boys are the ones wearing the trousers," I said.

"You're having me on, aren't you?" said Ronnie. I agreed that I was joking because I didn't want to seem an eejit. "A girl doesn't have a mickey," he said.

"Which girl doesn't?" I asked, surprised.

"No girl does, you eejit." There it was. I hadn't fooled him. Ronnie did think I was an eejit. "Don't you have a sister?" he asked. Yes, I did have a sister, but I'd never thought of her as a girl, really. She was just . . . well, just a sister.

"And did you never notice on bath night that she doesn't have a mickey?"

I had sort of noticed that all right, but if I'd thought of it at all, I probably assumed it would grow in later. The truth was, I couldn't remember when I'd first become aware of my own mickey. For all I knew, it hadn't been there to start with. I did remember one time waking up in hospital and being sore down there. Maybe they'd attached it in the hospital. No, 'cause then you could attach them to girls, too. So, boys had mickeys, girls had . . . what? I didn't know why, but this was all vaguely, uncomfortably . . . interesting. For a brief moment, before I copped myself on, I found myself thinking about the aggravating Assumpta Jordan. That was when the confusion got to me and – I just couldn't help myself – I bopped Ronnie on the snot.

Portobello Road, where I lived, had houses on only one side; on the other side of the road was the Grand Canal. The canal was as old as I was, maybe even older. From my earliest memories it was there, and the canal bank was my happy playground. Under my mam's suspicious eye at first, then with my pals and just the odd what's-he-up-to-now call from my mam on the doorstep, I explored the great outdoors of the Grand Canal bank.

The small house we lived in was very much like the other small houses on the road, except that some of them – ours was one – had tiny front gardens of hard-packed earth. The houses looked as though they had only one storey, but at the back there was an upstairs and a downstairs. Upstairs was a bedroom with one bed in it for my mam and dad, and one for me; downstairs was the kitchen, the scullery and the backyard with the lav at the end of it. What with the heat from the range that was always on for cooking and with the comforting smells of food, the kitchen was where we spent a lot of time. The scrubbed wooden table was pushed up against the window overlooking the walled, paved yard, where broad-leafed grass managed to struggle up between the cracks every spring. The table was usually covered with a shiny oilcloth which needed only a lick of a damp cloth to clean. Matching oilcloth skirted the mantelpiece. This mantel-cloth was cut up and down along the edge like saw teeth and was fixed to the front of the mantelpiece with thumbtacks. At each end of the mantelpiece

itself sat the china dogs guarding the tea caddy, the drum of salt and the Child of Prague in the middle, with the rent book behind him. Granma gave him to us along with the thrupenny bit that was put under him so that we'd always have money.

Off the hall, just inside the door, was the front room, which was the everything-else room. It was the sitting room; the room for Sunday dinner; the room where I was washed in the tin bathtub in front of the fire on Saturday night; the room where people who came to visit had a cup of tea, or perhaps a bottle of stout, or maybe even a glass of table wine at Christmas. It was the room where I could spread out my toys under the table and play – or listen, secret and quiet, while trying to make sense of the talk overhead. It was also the room where in fervent – if infrequent – spurts, the rosary was said in the evening. After my mam had done the women's retreat and was convinced we were all on the way to hell would be a busy rosary time. Harrington Street chapel was where the mams retreated, every night for a week, to be preached at by the visiting order, the Marists or the Redemptorists or whoever. The big guns, my dad called them. Apparently your eternal salvation was too important a thing to be left to the likes of the parish priest, so the big guns were needed to blast the cobwebs off your immortal soul.

During the day, the mams would all compare notes about the last night's sermon like they were judges giving the priests marks. "He had a nice voice, I thought," said one of the women.

"Nice voice, how are ya!" said another. "There's no point in keepin' it a secret to hisself that he has a nice voice. I was on'y halfway back in the chapel and I couldn't hear a word. I might as well have been listenin' to that Marcel Marceau."

Another said, "Jayzis, I nearly wet meself when he let that roar out of him. Put the heart crossways in me boozum with his describin' the torturin' tongues of spittin' hellfire, he did. Gave me goose pimples. Best I ever heard."

The men's retreat came the week after the women's, and it was the women's job – the priest told them so from the pulpit – to make sure the dads showed up, although I wasn't sure that all the dads went all the time. I saw mine and Scotty's dad heading off in the wrong direction entirely one evening, unless it was just going for a bit of a stroll before the chapel they were.

But there was no getting out of the rosary when my mam was weighted down by the sins of the household. Everybody knelt down then with rosary beads adangle while she orchestrated things. "The Five Sorrowful Mysteries," she'd call out and lead off the first mystery. Or the Five Joyful Mysteries, it might be. Although, sorrowful or joyful, they didn't sound to me any different from each other. You started with the Our Father, followed by a clatter of Hail Marys and a Glory Be, keeping score on your beads as you went. When you got all the way round the beads, you had won that round and were ready for the next.

With elbows on the seat, I surveyed the room through the bars of the chair back, a prisoner to prayer. My nails picked at the wallpaper beside me where it was beginning to flake along the join. As soon as my mam noticed that flaking, she'd start working on my dad to repaper the room. He'd start working on her to convince her that all it needed was a patching job – and he'd get to it as soon as he had the time – and could find a piece of wallpaper to match – and got the paste brush back from Mr Smith.

With the firelight behind it, the saggy armchair beside the grate had a fuzzy halo, a canonisation bestowed upon it by the raking claws of the stray cats that my mam would bring in to have a heat and a sup of milk – cats that my dad would scare out of the house again by flailing at the chair with a rolled-up newspaper. "Get out t'hell out o'that. Why do you let those mangy things into the house?" he'd ask my mam. "No wonder we have fleas."

My granda's comment on that was, "Oh, well, if ya have fleas, sooner or later y're bound to get cats."

My dad was kneeling now on one knee at the haloed chair, his head to its back, elbows sunk into the cushion; the sole of his shoe was worn almost all the way through in one spot. Another halo. The fire flickering on the hearth showed up the maze of meandering cracks and tributaries in the tiles from years of smashing Halloween nuts on them with the clothes iron. There sat the iron itself beside the fender, up on its end like a little dog, begging for any more nuts that might come its way. A small platform was attached to the grate where the iron – or the teapot – could be placed and swung in over the fire and kept warm. I gave a lead soldier a fiery end on that platform one time: swung in over the blazing turf, the British Grenadier buckled, melted and dripped slowly into the flames below for the honour and glory of Ireland.

The fireplace was the first thing to be attended to by my mam on a winter's morning before we got up. For safety's sake, because you never knew when a sneaky cinder might decide to come back to life and burn the house down, she would shovel the ashes from the grate into a heat-discoloured Jacob's biscuit tin. Then, before placing the fresh coal on its bed of crumpled newspaper and crossed sticks, she sometimes blackleaded the grate using an old toothbrush. The blacklead came in a tin with a zebra on it. Was it made from zebras, I wondered, like glue was made from horses? Or maybe it was for putting the stripes on the zebras.

The front room, having the only window that looked out on to the street, was also for waiting and watching. If someone was expected, you could keep an eye out for them and, before they even knocked, could have the door open for them – or not.

"Mam, Mam! The rent man is coming."

"Oh, Jesus! He didn't see you, did he?" She was downstairs at the table, rolling out potato cakes on the oilcloth. "Come away from the window," she said. Then with greater urgency: "Come on down here to the kitchen. Let's play a little game. The next knock we hear at the door will be . . . will be the Grim Reaper. So we mustn't make a sound and we mustn't let him in. Then we'll be safe."

"What's the Grim Reaper, Mam?"

"Shusht! Not now. In a minute." The unanswered rat-ta-ta-tat of the knocker was repeated. Another silence. Holding my breath, I looked up the stairs at the door. The knocking came again, louder; then it became a pounding as the brass knocker banged and banged so hard that I expected the whole door to explode inward in a shower of splinters. With an angry rattle, the letter box suddenly swung open to reveal the eyes of the Grim Reaper himself. Startled, I let out a yelp and leaped backward out of sight into the flour-covered arms of my mam.

A waspy, angry voice buzzed down the stairs. "I know you're in there, missus. I seen the boy. So, listen to me. I'll be back this evenin'. You'd better have somethin' for me then. You're way in arrears, you know that, don't you?" The letter box clattered shut, and the grey, watery eyes were gone. We sat together for some time, my mam and me, on the stone flags of the kitchen, not saying a word, the only sound the creaky swinging of the letter-box flap.

"Well, the old rip," my mam finally said. "I'm sure the whole street knows now."

"Knows what, Mam? That the rent man is the Grim Reaper?"

Her cheeks filled with air which she let out with a pop. "He'll be the death of me anyway, so he will, if your dad doesn't get some money for him somewhere. Blast him to hell." Who did she mean? My dad or the rent man? There was a slightly frantic note in her voice that I was hearing more often these days. A floury imprint whitened her forehead where it had rested in her hand. The mark of the Grim Reaper.

2

THE END

I COULDN'T READ yet but I was able to recognise that combination of letters, and they didn't seem to be in the right place. This wasn't where the book should end. If you were going to go to the trouble of reading all the way through a story, the ending shouldn't make you want to cry.

In pyjamas beside the fire, I had been snuggled up to my dad, listening as he read me the story of Robin Hood, a bit every night before bed. My mam on the other side of the fire had her hand stuffed deep into one of his socks she was darning. The back of her hand showed through a hole that got smaller and smaller as she went back and forth with a needle of wool, making the hole disappear. A hole was nothing, so my mam was making nothing disappear.

At least until he reached this bit of it, Robin Hood was the best story my dad had ever read to me. I thought they had the life, those Merry Men: Friar Tuck and Will Scarlet and Allan-a-Dale and Little John and Robin himself, eating roast venison and drinking mulled something as they sat around a campfire singing songs and always getting the better of the Sheriff of Nottingham and having fun doing it. Except that my dad had just read out where Robin gets old and, all weak and useless, shoots an arrow off into the forest and asks to be buried where it falls to earth. I couldn't believe it.

"But, Mam, why does he have to die?" I asked. She looked at my dad, who had taken his arm from around my shoulder and was examining the spine of the book very closely. Apparently deciding she wasn't going to get any help from that quarter, she said, "Because . . . well, because his life is over."

Not a satisfactory answer at all. My dad would know better. I squinted back across my shoulder at him. "But that's no reason, is it, Dad? What does that mean, his life was over?"

Pulling his eyes away from the book, he cleared his throat and, as casually as though he was discussing the weather, said, "It *is* a reason, son. The best reason. Sure, what else can we do when our lives are over only die?" If he expected me to be reassured by the innocent tone, I wasn't. Terror grabbed hold of me. After all, Robin Hood was only an Englishman, but what was being hinted at here was something monstrous altogether.

"But what . . . ? Does that . . . ? Mam, does that mean me dad is going to die?" It was almost a wail came from me. My dad nodded and worked his mouth as though it had been glued shut. My mam looked from one to the other of us and then threw her eyes upwards like she was looking for a pair of glasses on her forehead. My dad finally got his jaws opened.

"Sure, everyone has to die; that's the way of it." There, that explains it, doesn't it, his voice implied. But it didn't.

"What! Me mam as well?" It *was* a wail this time.

Scooping me up, my mam started there-thereing me and muttering about rubbishy books that shouldn't be read to children. "Bad enough," this to my dad, "that you have to open your mouth in the first place, but then to go and throw the hammer after the hatchet altogether. Now look at the child."

My dad did look at me – as though I tasted sour. He opened his mouth but quickly snapped it shut again. "Oh, well," he finally said with a sigh, "I think I'll go out for some cigarettes. And it's time you were in bed anyway," he said to me. He sounded cross now, as though my mam's bad mood was my fault. Her lips tightened into a straight line, but she didn't say anything as he went out the door.

It sometimes took my dad a long time to come back with his cigarettes, and when he did, he'd be in great form altogether, tickling my mam and singing soppy songs to her. But whether she was tickled when he came back this time I don't know, because by then I was well into a sleep of roaring dreams of arrows falling from the sky and turning into gravestones where they landed. Gravestones that had my name on them.

3

SOMEHOW THE CATS that came to visit seemed to know not to show up when my dad was there, and not to come all together either. One by one, at different times of the day, they showed up, in all shapes and sizes and colours and degrees of decrepitude. Enticed in by my mam with a bowl of milk and the promise of a better life indoors beside the fire, they'd stay until they began to wonder what they were missing outside or until my dad came home and hunted them out with a rolled-up *Evening Press*. My dad wasn't that gone on cats ever since the night when he was coming home after being out for cigarettes and he said one of them tried to run through the spokes of his front wheel and sent him flying, black and blue, over the handlebars. My mam wanted to know what colour the cat was; was it maybe a pink one? My dad did the thing with the back of his hands like he was shooing away flies or shoving sand away from in front of his chest before it covered him; then he buried his face in the paper and went deaf.

Cats didn't die; they had nine lives. Dogs hadn't and did. Bermo and me were prowling along the canal bank up past the Ever Ready factory and exploring among the reeds at the water's edge where you might find something interesting, a waterhen's nest maybe or a big roach mooching around the base of the reeds, but this day we found a dead dog. Murdered he was; tied to a rock and dumped into the deep, clear water by the lock gates at Richmond Street Bridge. Open-mouthed, we watched, as the dog, also open-mouthed, swayed gently from side to side at the end of his tether, a hairy sinner in a watery limbo reaching in vain for heaven.

Heaven. That's where they'd told me Robin Hood had gone. And heaven had it over Sherwood Forest any day, they said, trying to

convince me that Robin Hood was better off there than in a damp, old forest in England. True enough, heaven sounded as though it was great gas altogether and the best place to live. Although you wouldn't think so from the goings-on of people when somebody on the street died. Sweltering in the heavy black clothes that smelled of mothballs and made them look like walking inkblots, they'd be wailing and bawling, as if there was no such place as heaven. Sure, the time me and Bermo tried to send Mrs Fortune to heaven, there was ructions.

The black-bordered cards we found dumped among the reeds on the canal bank. We knew that a person got one of those cards pinned on his hall door when he died, like it was an invitation to heaven. RSVP. Reply Soon Very 'Portant. Obviously the guest list had been shortened this year and they had these invitations left over, but it seemed a sin somehow just to leave them lying around when there were people who could use them. We looked at the cards and then at each other, both thinking the same thing: Mrs Fortune. The oldest person on the road, Mrs Fortune was so ancient and wrinkled she looked like she was made of dried apples stacked on top of one another, and she already had a sort of dead smell about her, like musty geraniums. Sure, wasn't she long over-due for her invitation? Bermo went off to find John Stokes, who was six and claimed to be able to write. I went home to borrow the loan of my mam's pen. She heard me come in, so I had to borrow the pen from her to her face rather than from behind her back, which I would have preferred. Explanations can get slippery on you. "What in heaven do you want a pen for?" she wanted to know. I nearly said that *was* what I wanted it for – heaven – only I caught myself on in time. Like I said, slippery.

"John Stokes is going to teach Bermo and me how to write," I said – which was true enough in a way.

"He is, is he?" She sounded disbelieving, but she handed over her pen all the same. "And I suppose he's going to teach you Spanish after tea? Be careful with that pen of mine."

She wasn't as smart as she thought, though; John Stokes didn't speak Spanish. I asked him when he showed up, and he looked at me like I had only the one eye stuck in the middle of my forehead. "What would I want with Spanish?" he snorted. "If any Spaniards that come to Dublin want to talk to me, they'd better speak English."

Good job we'd found a pile of the cards, because John Stokes wasn't nearly as good a writer as he let on. Course he blamed the pen, saying it was a lousy speller with a cloggy nib, but my mam never had any trouble with it and wrote lovely letters. Hunkered down uncomfortably among the reeds on the canal bank, he took longer than expected, and we got through a half-dozen of the cards before coming up with one good enough to stick on the door. This finished article was lovely, though, not a bit smudged nor blotted, and with a nice verse we felt was the perfect blend of piety and optimism.

> *This morning around about seven*
> *Mrs Fortune went to heaven*

John Stokes had a straight pin stuck in the top of his lapel, and that would do to fix the card to the door. But who was to do the fixing? That was the thing. If we were seen near the house, we'd go right to the top of the list of suspects, and that wouldn't do at all.

Just then, like an answer to a prayer, didn't Jacko go by. Jacko, of course, wouldn't normally be considered the answer to anyone's prayers. A curse is more like it. Jacko's day consisted of a non stop series of lurches from calamity to catastrophe and back again. Like the time we were all playing in my front room. When she heard that Jacko was coming, my mam removed everything breakable from the front room before he was let in. It couldn't be safer, you'd think. But with Jacko there was no safe place. Somebody looked out the window and said Jacko's dad was coming. "Where?" says Jacko, poking his head out the window to see. Out the closed window. There was a sharp crack and a clatter of falling glass, and Jacko's head was sticking through one of the panes while the rest of him stayed inside on the sofa.

"Jayzis, Mary and Joseph," said Jacko's dad, stopping dead in the street outside. "Don't move!" Jacko wanted to know why not. "Because I'll bloody well skin y'alive if you do." He shouted to me to open the front door for him and then to go and get a towel. "And don't you move a muscle, ya little bollix," he yelled at his son.

Wrapping the towel carefully around Jacko's neck and head, his dad gently pulled all of him back into the room where everyone was laughing like mad. Everyone but Jacko's dad, that is. His face was as white as a rich man's shirt as he kept his eye on what window glass was still in position. We were all impressed into silence a second later when the top part of the broken pane came thudding down like a guillotine where Jacko's head had just been. Jacko himself went white now and started to cry.

"I'll give you somethin' to cry about, ya maggot," his dad said. "This is somethin' else I have to pay for out of me hard-earned wages, a new pane o' glass." Having taken Jacko's glasses off and stowed them safely in his own top pocket, he gave his son a clip on the side of the head with the back of his hand. "At least you didn't break your glasses this time," he said, giving him another skelp before marching him home by the ear. He came back with a piece of cardboard to block the hole in the window. "Tell your da I'll be back on Saturda' with the pane an' the putty," he said to me. "The car'board oughta hold her till then." The cardboard cut and in place, off he went, talking to himself. "Jayzis. One o' these days I'll be dug out of that young fella o' mine, so I will. There can't be another one like him in the whole o' Dublin. In the whole worl'." The door slammed him into silence, but we could see his lips still moving as he went homeward past the window with its new pirate's-eye-patch pane.

No, you wouldn't want Jacko anywhere near you most of the time – but under these circumstances it was decided the risk might be worth it. Surely even Jacko could be trusted to pin a bleedin' card to a bleedin' door without making a bleedin' bags of it?

"Jacko," called John Stokes. "Do us a favour, will ya?"

"Wot favour?" said Jacko.

"It's old Mrs Fortune's birthday. Just stick her birthday card on the door, would ya?" John Stokes could come up with good lies like that right off the top of his head.

Our eyes turned toward Jacko as he asked, "Wye don'tcha do it yerselves?"

Eyes swivelled back to John Stokes. "Because," he explained patiently, "it's a secret and we want to surprise her." Apparently this made sense to Jacko, because he ran off with the card, leaving John Stokes calling after him to fix the card to the centre of the door and then go straight home and not say a word to nobody. There was a squeal of brakes as a cyclist jammed on to avoid smashing into Jacko. Almost went over the handlebars, the cyclist did, ending up with his feet on the ground, the crossbar jammed up along his back, the saddle over his head and things raining down out of the saddlebag on top of him. His language was choice, and, ducked down among the reeds on the canal bank, we added some swear words of our own. It must be game over now. Surely everyone on the street would have heard that commotion. But when we looked up cautiously a moment later, the cyclist was turning down Bloomfield Avenue and Jacko was just opening Mrs Fortune's gate; nobody else was in sight.

Mrs Fortune's door mustn't have been properly closed, because it swung open on creaky hinges as Jacko pressed the pin in, and he staggered forward. Grabbing the doorknob to recover his balance, he now staggered backward, pulling the door shut with a bang. Waving frantically at Jacko to go away was only a waste of energy, because he ran for dear life in our direction and finished with a flying, squelchy jump into the reeds beside us. Hearts pounding, we listened for any sign he'd been twigged. Not a sound. Heads poked cautiously up. Everything was grand: the door was closed and the card was in place. All we had to do now was wait for the fun to start. And only that Jacko had left his stupid shoe behind him on the doorstep, we might have got away with it.

First into view was Mrs Cunningham. She was so busy rooting through her shopping basket and checking her list to make sure she'd got everything that she hardly gave Mrs Fortune's a glance. Four doors on, though, she stopped and looked up with a puzzled expression. It was like it was a long way from her eyes to her brain and the message had only just arrived. Scuttling back, she took another dekko at the door. Her hand fluttered to her mouth, to her head, down to her chest and back to her mouth again before it decided – as it was on the move anyway – it might as well bless her.

It did so with tight, hasty little movements, as though it was brushing away cobwebs as Mrs Cunningham looked up and down the road for someone to share the excitement with. There was nobody about so she headed for home instead at a brisk trot. A few steps on, though, she stopped, and we knew why. There was no point in her going home, was there? The only one who'd be there was old Mr Cunningham, and what use was he? He had gammy legs and talked real slow, saying each word about five times. "Walks with a stutter and talks with a limp," was what we said about him. No, better go somewhere else. Bermo gasped as, dashing back, she hammered on his door. His mam came out, her hands flew up to her mouth at the news, and then, holy God, didn't she go and bang on my door? Now there were three women running about like the Keystone Cops who took a door apiece and banged out three more women. Now they were six. And then they were twelve. I don't know why, but none of us had actually foreseen this development. The multiplying mob headed for Mrs Fortune's, growing larger with each banged-on door and transforming from a mob into a religious procession by the addition of rosary beads and prayer books and hushed tones. Some had even managed to equip themselves with blessed candles, like they kept them handy in the hallstand beside the bicycle lamp and pump, ready for just such an emergency.

When they got to Mrs Fortune's, they stopped and got the rosary beads going; some, those who had a scarf or something soft to kneel on, went to their knees on the footpath. Heads were bowed and hands clasped to bosoms as fingers inched their way along the beads. The low prayer murmur floated across to the reeds like the ominous drone of bees.

Next thing, didn't the door open and Mrs Fortune herself come out to see what was up. "Jayzis, Mary and holy St Joseph," said Mrs Carmody, the first to witness the miracle. With the shock, she drew in a gasp of air and almost swallowed her upper plate. Then she tripped over a kneeler behind her and sat down so hard on the footpath that all the air she had just taken in at such risk to her false teeth came out again in a noisy rush. Old Mr Costigan, who always prayed the loudest and the longest in the chapel, kissed the crucifix on the end of his beads and held it up at arm's length in front of him. "Depart from me, ya corset," he whined in his cracked, high-pitched voice – higher even than usual with the excitement of the moment.

They were all on their feet now, not sure if this wasn't indeed a miracle and that maybe Portobello Road would soon rival Lourdes as a place of pilgrimage, with cripples being dipped in the healing waters of the canal, when somebody said, "Come forth, Lazarus, but he came fifth and lost the race." This brought them back to earth and common sense took over. Of course, Mrs Fortune wasn't dead; wasn't she standing there in front of them? Balanced a bit wobbly on her canes, it's true, but still very much alive, her two eyes sticking out like a little dog's bollix in wonderment at what was going on. Manoeuvring on her sticks, she looked back at the door with her invitation to heaven pinned to it – and almost accepted it then and there. Somebody grabbed her as the canes fell sideways with the shock, and my mam ran in and brought out a kitchen chair for her to sit on. Mrs Barron, from next door, thought a drop of the Redbreast she'd put by for the Christmas was called for and ran back to get it. But when she came out, what with the lather of sweat she was in from rushing home and foostering in the back of the sideboard for the bottle, and the crush around Mrs Fortune that you'd need a battering ram to push through, and the fact that no one was looking at her anyway, didn't she drink the whiskey herself.

Everyone was talking at once now, *What*ing, and *Where*ing and *Why*ing out of them to beat the band. This gave way to a lot of, tsk, tsking and head shaking before silence fell and eyes began wandering about in search of the no-good brats behind all this. We were hunkered down now as low as possible in the reeds; any lower and we'd have been needing straws to breathe through. Then came a bloodcurdling cry of triumph – the hound catching a sniff of the hare – that made the reeds tremble. "That's my son's right shoe," cried out Jacko's mam. "I'd know it anywhere, the way he has the lace butchered into a Gordon knot."

I looked at Jacko's feet and for a moment thought, stupid though it was, that we were in the clear because Jacko had his right shoe on. Then I noticed that there was no shoe on the left foot.

Why would anybody expect Jacko to have his shoes on the proper feet?

There was some disagreement about what happened next. Jacko claimed we tried to drown him; we said he fell into the canal of his own accord when he heard the baying of his mother. But one thing was sure: the splash brought the religious procession flocking across to the canal where it miraculously converted back into a mob again – a mob that towered and glowered over us in the reeds. I felt like a roast chicken on a plate, waiting to be ripped apart and handed around. Help yerself to some o' his brains, why dontcha? He obviously doesn't use 'em. Jacko's mam seemed to take her time dragging him from the water, as if she was thinking she should maybe let him drown, so she should; that maybe it would be the merciful thing to do. Assembled on the grass we stood – me, Bermo and John Stokes shaking, Jacko dripping and shaking – waiting for the trial to begin.

The grabbing of your ear is such an intimate operation that it's normally carried out only by members of your own family, but this time it seemed to be understood that it was open season on ears. Each was grabbed by whoever happened to be closest to it, and its squirming owner followed as it was dragged across the road to Mrs Fortune's garden, which was to be the courtroom. Jacko said afterward that it was like the Spanish Imposition with everyone screaming at you from all sides.

"How dare ya, ya little brats?"

"Where'd you get them cards?"

"Whose idea was it?"

"Gurriers, that's what yez are, gurriers."

"The youngsters o' today."

"I don'know what Dublin is coming to." They ran out of steam and fell briefly silent before a kind word from Mrs Fortune got them started again.

"Ah, sure, they're on'y chislers," was all she had to say to open the floodgate again.

"That's no excuse."

"Weren't we all chislers once?"

"We never done the likes o' that."

"Where do they get it from?"

"I blame them picture houses."

And every time there was a slight pause, old Mr Costigan's thin voice piped in with, "Bring back the rod. That's what I'd do. Bring back the rod."

By the time it was all over, Jacko's clothes were nearly dry and I was nearly deaf. We were marched off individually, each by his own mam, to be punished according to the laws of his own house – home rule. I felt I got away lightly enough under the circumstances, managing to convince my mam I'd had nothing to do with it, that the whole thing was John Stokes's idea.

"You want to watch out for them older boys," she said. "They'll take advantage of you youngsters and get you into trouble." What could I say? Nothing, obviously. At least, not without getting myself into hot water. I let John Stokes take most of the blame, even though, when you came right down to it, his only crime was being able to write.

So, even though everyone said they wanted to go to heaven; and even though you couldn't get into heaven without dying; and even though heaven was supposed to be the happiest place in the world; death was no laughing matter. Death was real and death was earnest, and for all that the oul' wans were always on about a happy death, it seemed to me that most of them would prefer an unhappy life any day.

The one place where people didn't seem to mind death was the butcher's shop. The butcher's was full of dead things: sheep hanging in the window; a row of half cows or pigs dangling from hooks and dripping blood from the tips of their noses on to the sawdust floor; bloody bits of animals on dishes behind the glass front of the counter and on the chopping block behind. Indeed, in spite of all the signs of death about the place, Saturday morning at the butcher's could be a very lively affair.

Elbowing her way to the front of the crowd was a fat woman with a peacock's feather in her hat. "Would ya ever weigh that, Mr Heffernan," she said as she slapped a parcel on to the counter. Mr Heffernan, the butcher, distracted with everyone trying to get served at once, obliged. "It's nearly two pound, Mrs Baker."

Mrs Baker let an "Aha!" out of her and gave a pause to make sure she had the spotlight. Then she said dramatically, as though she was taking part in a play, "Do you know what it is? I'll tell ya what it is! It's the two-pound bone out of the four-pound roast you sold me for last Sunday's dinner, is what it is, ya chancer."

4

BY PRESSING A cheek against the front window and closing the room-side eye, you could stretch your view of the road. "Look at him at the squinty window," my dad would say. "Alec through the looking glass. Any closer to the window and you'd be outside looking in."

But there was one early morning he was as keen as me at the window. We were both in the front room with just the flicker of a fire going, the almost-darkness hovering about the deserted street outside. Every other minute, my dad was up to look out and then back again to the fire as he smoked one cigarette after another. Each deep drag made the red tip glow fiercely, as though he was trying to make the day brighter with his cigarette. The sun wasn't high enough yet to sparkle the canal. The water looked black, like a place the Loch Ness monster might come on his holiers: long shadows of the trees on the bank trailed into the water like flat snakes taking a drink. The morning air was cold enough that I could see my breath making little clouds that flattened out and fogged the glass in front of me.

"What can be keeping her, at all?" my dad said. He was just about to light a fresh cigarette from the butt of the old one when there came the clip-clop of horse's hooves and a stagecoach came into view. Cheek pressed to the window, I squinted down the street behind the horse-drawn cab; no sign of rustlers or Injins. With a "Whoa" and a haul on the reins from the man up on top, the cab stopped at our door.

"Oh, dear God in heaven!" said my dad, so exasperated that he threw the new cigarette into the fire, instead of the butt. "Couldn't they get her a proper taxi?" Coat-tails flying, the stagecoach driver jumped down to swing open the cab door as the horse lifted its tail and dropped round, brown apples that smashed open on the road and lay there steaming.

Inside in the dark of the cab, I could see my mam's white gloves and white face, like an Al Jolson poster. The shabby coach swayed on its big springs like a ship at the quay, and my dad reached up and helped my mam ashore. Carefully cradled in her arms was a blanket-wrapped bundle. My dad put coins into the outstretched, fingerless glove of the cabby, who looked, shook his head and thrust the glove out again. There was a bit of an argument, but having glanced at my mam, who wasn't paying a bit of attention, my dad jingled more coins from his trousers and handed them over. The cabby dragged the small suitcase he'd been holding hostage from the dark interior of the cab, slammed the door and swung himself upward like a monkey. "Giddy up," he said and flapped the reins. The horse snorted and shook his head like he was saying no, but he moved off anyway.

"Stop foostering," said my mam to my dad as they came into the house. He was carrying the little case and fussing around her and getting in her way. "I'm all right. I'm just going to lie down for a bit. Why don't you put the kettle on and bring me up a cup of tea?" Without looking – she was still smiling down at the bundle like it was something precious – she said to me, "Come and say hello to your wee sister." What was she saying? I didn't have a sister. Shaking my head, I stayed by the window with its familiar and reassuring view. My mam sighed and went up the short flight of stairs to the bedroom.

Little cooing sounds were drifting down as though she was talking gently to someone, but I knew she couldn't be because she was by herself, because my dad was downstairs in the kitchen, gathering the makings of the tea and calling up something new every minute. "Where's the tea caddy? – the matches, I can't find the matches – how many spoonfuls of tea should I put in? – I'll just put the sugar in the cup, will I?"

My mam didn't come down and take over as she usually would. She seemed content to lie upstairs with the bundle, listening to my dad making a shambles of the kitchen in the pursuit of a pot of tea. And all the while the banging was going on downstairs, I never moved from the window, just followed the action, bat-like, with my ears. I knew something important had happened, but I hadn't quite figured out yet that I was no longer an only and all that that meant.

The rattle of the lid going on the teapot told me that, at last, tea was made. Clinking up from the kitchen came my dad with the tray awkwardly balanced and the milk bottle at a risky tilt. He turned in the hallway and went out of sight again up the next flight of stairs to the bedroom. Along Grove Road on the other side of the canal, a lone cyclist slowly pedalled, his legs encased in brown canvas pull-ups against the rain that would surely come before the day was out. Nothing else moved. The sun had climbed high enough now to splash the surface of the canal with thin stripes of pale, runny-egg-yolk yellow, but the reeds at the bank still looked black and sharp and menacing.

I could hear all sorts of mushy sounds from upstairs and, once, a high whine like a cat or something. When at last my dad came down, the smile on his face didn't look real; it looked like a set of lips cut out of the Beano and stuck under his nose. Although he looked my way, I didn't think he was really seeing me. His eyes were squinty as though he was trying to focus on something off in the distance. The back door banged as he went down the yard to the lav. He could be there for a long time, reading the paper in a cloud of Gold Flake smoke.

I was still at the window when Jacko went by. His mam and dad must've still been in bed and he'd snuck out, because he wouldn't normally be let out by himself in the strangeness of the empty, early morning world. Wasn't he dangerous enough when the streets were full of people who could keep an eye on him? I didn't rap on the glass to get his attention, but he saw me anyway. He waved, a big grin on his face, his steel-framed glasses glinting in the pale sunlight. But now, with his face turned my way, he wasn't looking where he was going and didn't he slidder full length into the horse shite.

Him lying on his back, unmoving, arms and legs in the air like a beetle, trying to figure out what to do next, should have been funny, but I didn't feel like laughing. After a bit of a struggle, he managed to flip himself over and now was spread between his tippy-toes and the ends of his fingers as he tried to navigate himself clear without getting more horse shite on himself. I watched in a detached sort of way rather than with the glee the event called for as he crabbed himself sideways out of the mess. Bounding to his feet, he took up a pose with his palms up, head to one side for me to admire. TaDa! You see, he seemed to be saying. I got out without getting absolutely covered. Smart, amn't I?

Even though Jacko wasn't so smart as he thought – there was something that hadn't dawned on him yet – I couldn't get interested enough to want to stay at the window. The faint creakings and cooings that were coming from the bedroom had to be explored. Turning away, I made for the foot of the stairs without waiting to find out how Jacko would react when he realised that his glasses were still nestled in the middle of the mess he had so painstakingly crawled out of.

Carefully I stepped on to the first step. I had never noticed before how creaky the stairs were, but as I crept up now trying to be quiet, every step screamed out a warning that I was coming. Poking my head around the door, I examined the room. Wherever this sister was, she wasn't in my bed under the window, and that was a relief. The wardrobe cut off the view of my mam's head, but the lump I could see told me she was in bed all right. Creeping to the side of the wardrobe, I peered around it and got a shock. A worried-looking little boy with a pale face and red hair sticking up at the back like Indian feathers was gawking at me from the other side of the wardrobe. "Come here to me, son," said my mam, reaching out and pushing the wardrobe closed. The mirror on the inside of the door disappeared, taking my reflection into the darkness of the wardrobe with it. Now I could see my mam: she looked happy and weary and sad, all at the same time. The bundle was across her chest and her pyjamas were open. As I watched, a tiny hand like a doll's crept from the bundle and made for her throat, flexing its talons.

"Look out, Mam," I screamed. The hand stopped and withdrew, and a whimpering came from the bundle. Pleased at having saved her, I was mystified by my mam's reaction.

"Och, now," she said. "See what you've done. Frightened your wee sister." The whimpering from the bundle had turned to crying, and my mam seemed to be bothered by it. If she was to get bothered enough by it, maybe she'd send it back. I decided to frighten this sister every chance I got. What did they want with it anyway? They hadn't asked me. And they asked me about other stuff, new shoes and things. Course, new shoes were more important than sisters. Well, as long as they kept it out of my bed. But if the racket it was making now kept up, I'd never be able to sleep ever again, so what was the point of having a bed?

Back downstairs, the road outside the window was becoming more like its usual self as the day brightened. The eggy-yellow surface of the canal was now tinged with pink and reflected, upside down, the growing number of cyclists pedalling along on the other side of the canal. The squashed and slithered-upon horse apples outside the door steamed upward like incense, an offering to the new day. No doubt Mr Costigan or somebody would be along soon with a bucket to take it away for his roses. How is it roses smell so nice?

5

THE WINDOW OF our house was to the left of the hall door; Bermo's house beside us had its window to the right of the hall door. Other than that – and the colours of the doors themselves – the houses were exactly the same, with the same view out over the Grand Canal of Grove Road on the other side of it. The hall doors, one green and one red, were perched side by side on granite steps which every so often the mams would attack with basins of soapy water and scrubbing brushes and scrub until the flecks in them sparkled in the sun like a silver mine. Then they'd light up the fags and have a chat while guarding the steps until they dried.

And they watched like hawks, these step mothers did. You'd never get past them without a foot check. "Don't you dare put your muddy feet there, you. Well, all right, if you have to go to the lav. But jump over the step or I'll skin you." Bermo and me pondered the strangeness of this: how things you normally wouldn't be interested in doing – or not doing, as the case might be – become very difficult to not do, or do, once you'd been warned off. We'd be just itching now to get our feet muddy and walk in and out and over and along the steps, just because of a rule against it. But with the mams on guard, we knew better than to try, and so the only thing was to turn the whole thing into a jeer. Out we'd leap over the steps like we were flying; like we could clear a dozen steps if we had a mind to.

"Oh, indeed," said Bermo's mam. "A right pair of Nijinskys yez are."

Nijinskys? Whatever they were, they sounded massive. And obviously they could fly. We were so taken with the idea of these airborne creatures that, leaping through the canal-bank reeds with capes and wooden swords, we spent the next few days being flying Nijinskys. Not that we gave up playing cowboys and Indians; Nijinskys just took over for a while and became another game added to the list. There were less energetic games, of course. Trenches and caves excavated from the canal bank formed the war zones for lead-soldier battles. We went on Dinky-car safaris through the dense jungles of the long grass. Boats made from the broad reeds at the water's edge or folded pages of the *Irish Press* were launched in search of the source of the canal, sometimes with a battered, and therefore dispensable, lead soldier on board as navigator. And there were always the pinkeens of the canal to be caught in gauzy nets. Or if you found a dead dog stuck in the reeds, you could try counting the maggots that spilled out of its stomach and floated away, wriggling, toward the locks. You couldn't count them all though: you'd go cross-eyed; there were zillions of them. Marbles were played up and down the gutter from Lynch's shop at one end of the street to McCarthy's at the other and back again; and when the chestnuts came down, you went scouring the park for them and played conkers. With old bicycle wheels you could have hoop races along the road, at least until your wheel – no doubt tired of being beaten with a stick – escaped and dived into the canal. Every day on the canal bank was fresh and new and as interesting as the one before, and life was perfect. And then suddenly it wasn't.

I don't what came over my mam to come home that morning with a baby. Why did things have to change? Oh, I still had the canal bank, no babies there, but the house rules had changed. Whereas before there hadn't been any restrictions, now I was for ever being told to do this, not to do that, to mind the baby, to keep quiet, to not jump down the stairs, to not play ball in the house. And all this because I was no longer an only child. But, if I was no longer an only, I had become something that was maybe even better. An oldest. At least that's what Bermo and me told each other – he was beginning to be plagued by babies also. The common enemy we had in babies made us pin-pricked blood brothers, and we checked each day on the news from the home front. "Any more babies in your house, Bermo?" I'd ask.

"I don't think so. Though, there might be, but. I heard strange noises from me mam an' dad's bed last night, all right. Haven't seen nothin' yet though."

"It's great to be the oldest though, in'it?"

"Oh, deadly."

"Massive."

Bermo's mam, though, seemed to have her own ideas about oldests, and she knew everything. At least, so my dad said. He'd throw his eyes to the sky when he came home and found her down in the kitchen with my mam; he'd go into the front room then and be real busy with rent books and things until Bermo's mam took herself off.

"Ah, to be sure," she was saying as she sat in the kitchen with my mam. "They're grand little chisellers, the pair of them. But the first-born, you see, is always a bit strange, a little" – she did a fluttery thing with her hand – "bockety. The others'll have an easier time of it, you'll see."

What did she mean, others? Surely my mam had learned her lesson? She wasn't going to be bringing home more babies, was she? Wasn't the one we had enough trouble? I watched and listened a bit longer, hoping to find out more about this baby business. Maybe I could pick up a clue as to how to put a stop to it. Or I might hear something else of interest. You sometimes heard interesting things if grown-ups didn't know you were listening. But today they were only on about the pictures. Bermo's mam, who saw all the new pictures, had been to one last night at the DeLuxe. It was about a six-foot rabbit that was invisible. That one sounded like a real waste of money. Imagine paying in to see a picture about a rabbit you couldn't see.

6

I DECIDED I might as well make the most of the way things were, as it seemed like we were stuck with the sister situation. Surely being the oldest had at least some consolations. For one thing, I had a head start on making myself the favourite with uncles and aunts and other old people. Whatever about my mam and dad being distracted by the baby and saying they didn't have time to play right now, aunts and uncles could be very generous with their time – and their spondulicks. You could often count on a little money changing hands when you met them. "Here, go and get yourself a few sweets," they'd say with a wink.

"Janey Mac, thanks very much." I'd slide the coins politely into the pocket for examination later – my dad said it was rude to stare at money like you'd never seen any before. And I wouldn't have to split it with any babies. I could splurge it all on Fizz Bags, or Lucky Bags, or Sailor's Chew, or Jelly Babies, or Cleeve's Toffee, or gob-stoppers, or Honey Bees, or Nancy Balls, or toys. Although, when it came to something to play with, I didn't always need toys, because there were things around the house that were sometimes better. Going about on all fours in the gasmask I found in the bottom of the sideboard, I was an elephant. Or using one of my dad's bicycle clips as an earring and with my mam's scarf tied on my head, I was a pirate. With one of the clips dangling from my nose, I could charge at people like a mad bull. Or be a pygmy. Pygmies were little black lads who lived in the jungle and ate people. Except clowns – my dad said they wouldn't eat clowns because they tasted funny. Pygmies didn't wear much in the way of clothes and shot poison darts at you through pea shooters. I could do that. Black shoe polish and two of my dad's handkerchiefs knotted around my waist would do the job very nicely.

When I was finished, I felt like a real poison pygmy. And it fooled my mam. She screamed in terror and dropped a plate into

smithereens when she saw me. "Amn't I afflicted? What will I do
with him?"

This wasn't the reaction I had expected. Applause was more
what I had in mind, and when she didn't start to laugh, I became
worried, thinking that maybe I'd done too good a job. "It's all
right, Mam," I said, trying to calm her. "It's only me. I won't eat
you."

"What have I got here at all at all?" she wanted to know, not a
bit calmed. I panicked and threw my arms around her legs,
screaming, "It's me! It's me! Don't send me to Africa. I'm afraid of
lions and tigers." I squirmed and pleaded into her apron until I
was white in the face. Next thing I knew, it was the tin bath, lots of
sudsy water and rough scrubbing. My mam with suds up to her
elbows was blowing her hair away from her face, first out of one
side of her mouth then the other, and telling me she'd take the
hide right off of me if she had to and to hold still in the name o'
God.

Just inside the front door was the hallstand. A glut of coats, capes,
caps, umbrellas, handbags and who-knows-what hung from it, like
it was a strange sort of hedge grown wild. In a compartment with
a hinged lid on it – I had to stand on tippy-toe to reach inside –
were the bicycle lamp and pump. And those cycle clips. My dad
used them to keep his long trousers from being chewed to flitters
by the chain wheel. And he could have them as far as I was concerned. The sou'wester and the pull-ups for cycling in the rain
were in there too, as well as the little tool bag you could strap to
the back of the saddle. There was also a small burping oilcan to
keep the chain from rusting and the brakes from seizing up. And
a cleaning rag to mop up when the oilcan got over-avaricious.

My dad was adjusting the front brake rod of his Raleigh with a
special tool from the tool bag. All holes this tool was, like metal-
eating moths had been at it. But it was designed that way, said my
dad. Each nut on the bike could be tightened with one of the
holes of that one tool. All for one and one for all, and every nut
for himself.

"I cycled all over Ireland before you were born," my dad said to me, patting the saddle like the bike was a dog and he was saying, "Good boy." He'd just got it upright again having fixed a puncture in the back wheel.

"I used never get so many punctures in the past." He bent down for a closer look. "No, they don't make tyres like they used to," he said. "Not nearly as good as the old ones."

"Why don't you get some of the old ones, then?" I asked.

"Sure aren't they long gone, didn't they use up all the rubber in the war against the Nazis?" I didn't think it could have been much of a war if they were fighting it with only tires and tubes. A funny, drawly word that, Naa-zzies.

My dad pushed forward on the handlebars while pulling the front brake lever, and the bike reared its back wheel into the air like a bucking bronco. Satisfied with the adjustment, he patted the saddle again and went down to the kitchen for his tea. I looked at the bike with new interest. It was leaning innocently against the hallstand, not showing any sign at all at its wartime experiences. For the bikes must be together at the rising of the moon. "Naa-zzie," I whispered accusingly at it before following my dad down the stairs to my mam in the steam-filled kitchen.

7

SOME TIME AFTER the death and resurrection of Mrs Fortune, I was sneaking through the bushes in St Stephen's Green trying to get close enough to a sparrow to sprinkle salt on its tail. If you put a pinch of salt on a bird's tail, it won't be able to fly and you can catch it. The round box the salt came in had a picture on it of a boy with a salt cellar chasing after a bird, proof positive they could be caught that way. And, further proof, the birds themselves were afraid of the salt and always flew away before I could get close enough to hit them with a pinch of it. Tiptoeing around a tree, I suddenly froze with one foot in the air – very like a salt-sprinkled sparrow myself. An arrow was stuck in the ground. Robin Hood's grave! Heart pounding, I went crashing back through the bushes, unsalted birds flapping away in all directions. Reluctantly my mam surrendered the deckchair she had just paid tuppence for and came with me to see dead Robin Hood.

It wasn't an arrow at all – only a thin, straight shrub with a few leaves on the end of it reaching up from the gloom toward the light. I felt a right eejit; and now, of course, as all the salt was spilt, I could forget about sprinkling sparrows. And my mam could forget about sitting in the sun, because she said she didn't have any more pennies to be so *flaithiúil* with on another deckchair. So, saltless and chairless, it was back to Portobello Road with the pair of us. *Flaithiúil* had a gas sound to it. And whatever it was, you could have it for tuppence.

The drum of salt was kept on the kitchen mantelpiece, and I could reach it by standing on a chair. Because I always dragged the chair back to its place, my mam never noticed the salt going – until the day I thought I'd try something new. "Glory be t'God. He's away with the whole box this time. Why did you ever tell him that story? Come back here out of that. No, son, you don't need all that. Unless you want to bury the bird. No, no, you don't, honest. Just a little bit of salt in a twist of paper will do you for a sparrow."

But not for a swan it wouldn't. The swans were so huge you'd need the whole box to sprinkle them to earth, and that's what I'd wanted to try. Every year at nesting time, a pair of swans would stake out a bit of the canal along Portobello Road for themselves. Woe betide any foreign swan that tried to park there – even for an instant. Then a terrifying, beak-bashing, wing-smashing battle would take place, which always ended with the gatecrasher flapping madly away down the canal and the victor in pursuit, snapping savagely at tail feathers. More than once, the posh people of Rathmines, on the other side of the canal, had their telephones disconnected as those powerful wings snapped the phone wires that were strung across the water at the end of our road. The telephone people tried to solve the problem by putting corks along the wires to stop the swans bashing into them. Spanning the canal banks, the corks looked like the dots and dashes of Morse code. I wondered would the swans get the message.

"Where did they get all them corks, Dad?"

"Left over from the Post and Telegraph men's lunches, most likely," said my dad.

"Will we ever have a telephone, Dad?"

"Sure, look! The way those telephone men work, if I was to apply now for a phone, I'd be long gone out of it, and you'd be old and grey, before they showed up. And they probably wouldn't have the right tools with them when they did come. Sure, we're fine the way we are."

If the swans were snarky most days – and they were – they were really vicious while their babies were small. "Stay away from them lads," old Mr Costigan wheezed. "Specially wen they got their lil' singlets wid 'em. Oh, they'd have yer goolies off ya in a flash, them lads." I puzzled about that for a bit and then questioned my dad, but it seemed he didn't know what goolies were either. But he said he'd have a word with Mr Costigan about it, oh yes indeed. He did agree though that Mr Costigan was right about staying away from the swans at nesting time. "It's only to be expected," he said. "They're just protecting their young. It's natural."

"Did you have to protect me when I was little?"

"Certainly we did. The tinkers were always coming by, trying to steal you. We had to beat them off with the frying pan many's the time." I could believe that tinkers would do the likes of that, because that was another book my dad had read to me by the fire, *The King of the Tinkers.*

When the baby swans were big enough, the mammy and the daddy swans took them out for a float to show them off. Come on now, let the people have a gawk at you. Look where you're goin'. Hold yer sister's wing. Clean yer face, ya little maggot, you've got canal muck hangin' from yer beak.

Sometimes I would manage to cadge a slice of a turnover from my mam to feed to the swans. "Well, all right," she'd say. "But only one slice, mind. It's not in the swan-feeding business we are."

Trying to make the one slice of bread last as long as possible, I tore it carefully into tiny pieces. One crumb to this swan, one crumb to that swan, until they began to make testy little hisses and close in on me. To my great surprise, I suddenly realised I could tell what the swans were thinking. Their mad, beady eyes were measuring the distance. Never mind the bread, they were telling each other, go for the little runt that's holdin' it. There's enough eatin' on him to do us till Christmas. With a yelp, I threw the remaining bread at them and fled.

When the little swans grew bigger, it was a battle ground all over again, because the parents got fed up looking after them and tried to run them out of it. Just like my mam sometimes told me – would I ever, for the love o' God, get out from under her feet and go out and play. But my mam would let me come back. The swans wouldn't. They'd hunt the young ones away down the canal a couple of times, and the young ones would come back a couple more times. Up and down the canal they'd go till it was busier than Dublin Airport with landings and takeoffs. Some more posh telephone conversations would end in mid-sentence with the downbeat of a powerfully passing wing. "The Hunt Ball this year was a disaster with all the . . . Hello . . . Hel . . . Operator . . . Operator . . ."

Like the swans, Bermo and me had our own stretch of canal which we rarely went beyond. Bounded by Lynch's shop at one end of Portobello Road and McCarthy's shop at the other, we felt that was enough territory for the two of us to patrol. Not that we'd try to hunt anyone away for coming on to the street or anything, but strangers were certainly noticed. Especially the odd-looking man with the ringlets and the hat like a flying saucer.

"Little boy," he asked me. "You would do for me a favour for sixpence?" Would I? For sixpence I'd even wear my own hair in ringlets.

"You will come with me, please?" The man led the way along the canal, down Bloomfield Avenue, into a side street and through the door of a dark little house. I followed a little nervously as the man went into the kitchen, but the thought of the sixpence gave me courage. "You will put on this light for me, please?" he said, pointing. "And the hall light? And outside the back door you will find a coal bucket. Some coal you will put in the grate for me like a good boy, and maybe work the poker?"

I didn't see any women in the house and presumed the man didn't have a mam of his own to riddle the fire and light the light, but how odd that a man his age never learned to do those things for himself. But that was my good fortune. I did as I was asked – it was dead easy – and took the sixpence happily. Very happily! Because my own pocket money was only fourpence, and I had to be good all week for that. From then on, after I'd had my tca, I was outside in the street before dark trying to look like the most efficient light-switcher-on-er and coal-putter-on-er in the world.

8

I N THE DISTANCE beyond Lynch's corner, the battery factory sat right on the water's edge. Oodles of black dust and lead battery casings and cardboard with Ever Ready printed on it in red and black spilled across the reeds and into the water from the factory dump. If you went that far fishing for pinkeens, with all the black dust around, you'd come back looking like a coal man; nothing white but your eyes. Then you could do the Minstrels: Mammy, how I love ya! How I love ya! Except that your mammy wasn't always in the mood to find this funny.

"Look at the cut of you! Get those things off at once." Then the tin bath and the carbolic soap would be hauled out and the big black kettle plonked on the range. Beside the fire in the front room, you'd be stood up in the bath and decarbonised while some of your friends would maybe be looking in the window at you and laughing. And you mortified and trying to cover your mickey casually with your hands without seeming to – your mam not giving a tinker's damn. "Would you ever stop squirming and hold the soap while I sluice you down."

For washing yourself in our house, that was it, the tub by the fire in the front room. The lav at the end of the backyard didn't have a bath in it, just the toilet. It had a door that didn't fit properly so that a wind came in under it and fluttered the squares of newspaper stuck on the nail on the back of it. The tin roof pounded like thunder in the rain, rain that sometimes blew in over the top of the door to go with the gale coming under the bottom. So that you wouldn't have to go down there in the middle of the night, there was always the pot under the bed in case you had to do a wee flood or a wee job.

Once I snuck downstairs from bed when my dad had gone out for cigarettes and in the firelight saw my mam standing up in the tin bath with no clothes on, washing herself. I couldn't see her

mickey, she was that sooty between her legs. Had she been down to the Ever Ready factory, or what? Sometimes it was just her feet she washed, and afterward she'd work away at a big bump on the side of her foot with a razor blade, paring her corns. For all that it made me shudder, it was fascinating to watch the blade sawing back and forth and flakes of skin falling to one side like a small version of the ham slicer in the butcher's. And sometimes the blade went into a razor for her to shave her legs. But my dad shaved his chin.

"I think I'd better stand up close to the razor this evening," he'd say, scratching at his chin like sandpaper. Then the razor would be brought down from the top shelf where it was kept out of the way because, although it was called a safety razor, my mam said it was a dangerous thing to leave lying around. A steaming basin on the kitchen table, the little mug that held the soap and shaving brush beside it, a mirror against the window, the curtains pulled back for extra light, and the stage was set. My dad attacked his grizzled chin with the soapy brush like he was beating an egg. The faster he went, the frothier the foam became until he looked like Santa Claus frothing at the mouth. Then the razor began ploughing soapy furrows up chin and down cheek. My dad always held his nose between the finger and thumb of his left hand when scraping at his upper lip, as though he didn't like the smell of the razor. Sometimes there'd be an "Ow" from him, followed by a muttered something that I couldn't quite hear, and then a little spot of red would seep through the whipped-cream whiteness of the soap. A corner ripped off the *Irish Press*, licked and stuck on the bloody nick would stop the flow.

Because he wasn't, as he said, made of money, my dad would try to make the blade last as long as possible, but eventually, with tears in his eyes, he'd decide that, expense or not, a new one was called for. Covered in soapsuds as my dad was, I would be sent out to Lynch's for it.

"A bugle-ette, please, Mr Lynch."

"Well, well! A Blue Gillette blade, is it? Don't tell me you've started to shave already?"

"No, it's for me dad."

"Your dad, is it? And I suppose you're helpin' him at it. Moppin' up the blood an' all. Ah, you're a good boy, so you are. Here." He'd open the glass lid on the box of broken biscuits and gesture with his chin. "Take a few."

Back in the kitchen, my dad might have forgotten about shaving and be engrossed in the back page of the paper, underlining words in pencil and doing sums in the margin. "It's a long shot, but if it came in, boys-o-boys but we'd be on the pig's back, what? Just leave it there, son. Thanks." He'd point vaguely at the table with the chewed end of the pencil and go back to his calculations, the soap drying to a grey scum on his chin.

Examining the wrapping on the blade with its picture of the moustached Mr Gillette on it, I thought it must be a wonderful thing to be able to shave. I couldn't wait. Then I'd be a man. Because it was only men that got to shave their chins. Women and girls and boys didn't. That was something to look forward to, the day I joined the nicked-neck brigade. Reaching under my dad's arm, I tore a bit off the newspaper, sucked it, stuck it on my chin and muttered, dadlike, into the neglected shaving mirror. My dad, engrossed in his dream of a fortune on four legs, didn't notice. Placing Mr Gillette face up on the table where he could catch my dad's eye, I went upstairs to stash the rest of the biscuits under the pillow so that I wouldn't waste away from night starvation while waiting for my beard to grow.

9

"I'M AFTER BORRYIN' the loan of me dad's bike," said Jacko. Jacko was teaching himself to ride a bicycle. His dad, of course, wasn't aware he was lending his bike for these lessons. Jacko thought it prudent not to mention this fact, because that machine was his dad's pride and joy, for ever being shined and oiled and pumped and patted, and wasn't for lending out to the mangling likes of Jacko – but dads didn't always want to know everything. They were quite likely to say, "Not now, tell me later, I'm busy," when you did try to tell them something, so it made sense not to burden them with too much info. Especially info that might rebound on you later.

With me and Bermo tagging along, Jacko scooted the bike along the canal as far as the bridge at Harold's Cross, where there was a slight slope that would give him a bit of a start. "Watch me now," says he, sounding full of himself as he pushed off from the top of the slope. He often started out like that, full of himself – and ended up emptier than a punctured balloon.

Being too small to get his leg over the saddle, he propelled himself by scrunching down under the crossbar, feet in the pedals, hands above his head on the handlebars. Legs pumping away goodo, he was getting up a bit of speed and, delighted with himself, he flashed down the slope, laughing. But then the laughing stopped. The balance of the bike was wrong or something, because things weren't going as planned. The bike was edging over toward the right the whole time. Toward the canal. Now it was off the road and on to the path along the water's edge; then it was off the path on to the grass and still heading at a slant for the water. He couldn't stop because he couldn't get a good pull on the brakes from that angle. His face was in such a lather of sweat that his glasses fogged up, and now he couldn't see where he was going. Into the canal was where he was going. And he was fast approaching the point of no return.

"Jayzis! What'll I do?" he screamed.

"Jump!" I roared through cupped hands. "Jump, or you'll be drownded for sure."

As the front wheel departed this earth, Jacko dived sideways for the reeds and left the bike to manage on its own. It didn't do too bad for a riderless bike, either. On it went toward the deep water, managing to keep itself upright, the pedals continuing to turn like an invisible man was on it. Lower and lower in the water it sank until, finally, all you could see of it was the handlebars and the saddle. I took a deep breath as though it was me was going under and watched, appalled, as the bike sank from sight out in the middle of the canal. The silence that followed lasted a long time. Jacko was sitting in the shallow water among the reeds with his steel-framed specs dangling from one ear, looking like a toy with a broken spring. Me and Bermo looked at each other, white-faced and silent at the magnitude of the catastrophe.

It was Bermo who finally broke the silence. "Jaaayzis," he breathed, his mouth hanging open. After another long pause he added, "Wot'll you tell yer da?" Jacko and me looked at each other; we knew, even if Bermo didn't, that there was no question of telling nobody nothing. The disappearance of the bicycle would have to become, like a decade of the rosary, a mystery. A sorrowful one in this case, for Jacko's dad was going to be rightly banjaxed for getting into work in the morning. Out on the calm water of the Grand Canal, a couple of bubbles from the shipwrecked bicycle broke the surface and popped with a sound like the blowing of goodbye kisses.

10

"WHEN SOMETHING IS good, you say it's deadly."
"I see," said my dad, but from the hesitant tone of his voice it didn't sound like he did. He had just given me a piggyback up to bed, and when I said it was deadly, he looked confused.

I started to explain. "If I seen a good picture at the Prinner . . ."

"Saw," said my dad. "Who's Deprinner when he's at home?"

"The Prinner?" My dad could be really thick sometimes. "The Prinner is the picture house in Rathmines. You brung me there last week," I said.

"Oh, The Princess. I see. Brought, not brung."

". . . and the picture we saw, *Scara . . . Scarasomething*, that was deadly. All that fencing." I rushed on because these interruptions were likely to take the conversation off in another direction and I wouldn't get my explanation out. "Or rapid. Something deadly is also rapid. Or massive. You can also say massive."

"Ah," said my dad. "So something deadly-rapid-massive would be three times as good?"

"You don't say that, Dad. It's either rapid or it's deadly or it's massive. They don't go together like that." I tried them out in my head, just in case – unlikely though it was – he might have something there. Rapid massive deadly. "No," I said. "It sounds bockety."

"Bockety?"

"Yes. Don't you know what bockety is?"

But he did know. "The pram's front wheel is bockety," he said, making a sour face as though it was something to be ashamed of. I thought it was deadly the way the wobbly wheel made a tockata-tockata-tockata sound as it was going down a hill with my mam fighting to keep it from running off the footpath and out in front of a bus. That'd be interesting.

"Jacko is real bockety," I said.

"How do you mean, son?"

"Well, the way he keeps bumping into lamp-posts, and slidin' into – I mean, falling down, and breaking things, and . . . and . . . well, he's just bockety, isn't he?"

"Oh, well, every cripple has his own way of dancing."

"Dancing? I never seen him dancing."

"Saw him. You never saw him dancing."

"I know. Didn't I just say that?" He could be really exasperating at times.

"I just mean, I suppose you're right. I suppose he is a bit bockety. If it comes to that, I dare say we're all a bit bockety." He gave an amused snort. "Yes, bockety's the word all right. You, me, your Aunt Lily, your mam, the pope, the whole world. Bockety."

"Sure, how could the pope be bockety? Isn't he inflammable?"

He laughed. "I dare say there's many an Orangeman from your mam's part of the country would love to have a go at proving that one. I think the word you want is infallible."

So many words. And still, with all of them, I didn't know what people meant half the time. Orange men? I hadn't heard of them before. Why were they called that? Was it because they were round? Or because they were yellow? And were there apple men as well? And banana men?

"And what if the pope does know everything?" my dad said. "Sure, that's enough to make anyone bockety. The only people who aren't bockety are the ones who don't worry about anything. And the only people who don't worry about anything are simple-minded, and you can't get more bockety than that, can you?" I tried not to, but I couldn't help giving him a pitying look. My dad laughed again. "You're a panic, so you are," he said. "Go to sleep, you bockety little boy." He tucked the covers up and rumpled my hair before going downstairs.

Sitting up again, I smoothed down my hair and, elbows on the windowsill, leaned my forehead against the cool glass. Bockety! I wasn't bockety, I knew I wasn't. Not like Jacko. I wasn't always banging into things like Jacko. Or losing things. Jacko couldn't be sent out for a bottle of milk without there being a good chance of him losing the sixpence. Even his pocket money, the thing you guarded with your life, wasn't safe.

Take that day outside McCarthy's shop. Down below in the shadows under the grating, among the rubbish – thrown-away sweet papers, cigarette packets, lollipop sticks, betting stubs, butts, bus tickets, empty match boxes – a shilling glittered tauntingly at us. Bermo was working away on a big wad of chewing gum in his mouth. The wad was so big that his jaw got tired and he handed it over to Jacko to finish chewing for him. When it was good and sticky, Bermo wrapped it round a piece of string and lowered it down through the grating. The idea was to hover the gum over the shilling and then drop it smartly straight down so that it stuck to the coin. Bermo and me took turns dabbing for the shilling; Jacko wasn't let near the precious string. After twenty minutes, though, both our faces were criss-crossed with grating marks, we were slick with sweat, the gum was black with dust and the shilling – which had clung to the gum for one brief, heart-stoppingly tantalising moment – was back on the ground. In exasperation, Jacko now grabbed the string and threw himself face down on the grating. And that was when he lost the last two of his four pennies pocket money.

Clattering out of his jacket, the copper pennies tumbled through the bars of the grating to join the shilling below. Things were really serious now. The way things had been, if we'd managed to get the bob, that was a plus. With his own money down there, what Jacko had now was a serious minus. With the dedication born of desperation, he worked away for ages with the string, and when he finally gave up, he said he was keeping the chewing gum as compensation for having lost the best part of a week's money.

"You're not going to eat that?" says Bermo.

"Why not?" says Jacko.

"It's been down the bottom of the gratin'," says Bermo.

"I don't care," says Jacko.

"And it's got fluff and stuff stuck to it," says I.

"I don't care," says Jacko.

"Maybe some oul' fella spat down the grating and the chewing gum landed in the gollier," says Bermo. Jacko paused for a minute

at that. Having examined the sticky wad carefully, he crossed the road and rinsed it off in the canal.

"Good as new," he said, popping it into his mouth.

Bermo, who'd been holding back for just this moment said, "Or there might be rat shite in the middle of it."

Even for Jacko, that thought was too gruesome. The chewing gum flew from his mouth and hit the side of McCarthy's shop with a thwack. There it stuck for a long moment like a pink snail, unsure which way to go, before it made up its mind and slid down through the iron bars of the grating for the last time. Jacko got a new nickname that day. He was called Rat Shite Boy for a long time after that.

11

I N THE EARLY dark of the winter's evening, the distant sounds from outside carried very clear: the gentle flap of washing on a line, washing that by morning would be frozen stiff like salted fish; the slam of a backdoor followed by the softer thud of another door as somebody went to the lav at the end of a nearby backyard. The fingernails of my left hand gouged ridges through the frost swirls on the inside of the window as I lay in my bed, covers up around my ears, nothing exposed but my nose and that left arm.

There was a great view from this window on washdays. If it was a day with a bit of a wind, the backyards looked like the Spanish Main, with sheets all aflutter like billowing sails, the creak of clothes lines like rigging in the wind. I was a pirate then, scanning the horizon through a rolled-up copy of the *Dandy*. Enemy cats on the starboard bow. Stand by to propel boulders. From here you could see the backs of the houses on St Kevin's Road. Once I saw a man and a woman dancing in the bedroom of the house beyond our garden wall. It must have been summertime and hot, because they had no clothes on.

My mam, too, took her part in the washday Armada. Pots and kettles of water were put to boil on top of the kitchen range on washday. If the weather was fine, the knobbly washboard, the block of carbolic soap and the tin tub were dragged out into the backyard. If I didn't have more important things to do, I'd help by taking one end of a sheet while my mam held the other, and we'd twist in opposite directions until all the water was wrung from it. Except you wouldn't do that with the one that was made of stitched-together flourbags for fear it might rip. Faded, but still legible, there was good reading yet on that sheet as long as it was treated gently. When the line was drooping full and before everything got manky dirty from trailing on the ground, it was hoisted into the air on a notched pole, and our backyard, too, was under full sail.

But on a cold night like tonight, any clothes left on the line froze rigid. Bermo's dad's overalls on the line next door would look by morning like someone squelched by a steamroller. I liked to stand my frozen pyjama legs by the fire and watch as the heat made them slowly collapse like the Chap's pal dying in slow motion in a cowboy picture. The Chap himself never got shot – well, maybe a flesh wound sometimes – but the pal sometimes did, and this always made up the Chap's mind for him to go after the bad lads and leave the girl – which we all agreed was only as it should be. "They got me, partner," the pal would go as his six shooter slipped from his weakening fingers. One knee sags but he's still half upright. Then the other one buckles, and he sprawls face forward in the dust at the fourpenny rush at the Prinner.

That's what it cost to get into the Prinner on a Saturday afternoon: four pennies; and you could pay all or part in jam jars if you wanted. A jam jar was worth a ha'penny. What would they do, I wondered, if everyone showed up one day with no money, only jam jars? Inside in the cashier's cage, the woman would be perched way up on a pile of jam jars, having to reach down with her big toe to press the button that made your ticket spit out of its brass slit at you. And what happened to all the six shooters dropped in the dust? Because you never saw anyone pick them up. The Wild West must be littered with guns: like the phone boxes must be full of Clark Kent's clothes.

Flexing my cold trigger-finger, I pulled my hand away from the frosty pane and in under the warm covers. It wasn't only clothes would freeze in the winter; sometimes the pipes would, too, and you'd have no water. Then my dad or mam would go out into the backyard and run a lit candle under the copper pipe fixed to the wall. In the kitchen, I'd have my ear to the tap. If they got lucky with the candle, I'd hear a faint hiss and be able to yell out encouragement. A puff of steam came next, then a reluctant trickle of water, followed by the full, gushing stream. Sometimes, though, things were beyond heat. One time, through the window, I saw my mam just standing staring at the wall, the lit candle hanging from her hand, dribbling its grease on the ground. I went out and saw a gash in the copper pipe with a spike of frozen water sticking out of it like a dog's tongue.

Before even a thimbleful of water could be heated on washday, the cast-iron range in the kitchen had to be fired up; and sometimes, if the paper was screwed up too tight or the sticks were damp, it was hard to get it drawing right. Then a double page from the newspaper would be spread open against the grille. There'd be the sucking roar as air rushed up the chimney, pulling the sparks into flame behind that newspaper. The trick was to hold the paper just long enough to get the fire going but not so long that it burst into flame itself. And the excitement when it sometimes did. On the hearth then, a wild dance on the burning paper would cause blackened crisps of it to float through the air of the smoky kitchen. Crisps that all had to be accounted for in case there was a bit of dangerous life left in any of them.

But when everything was going like billyo, with the fire drawing well and the wash water bubbling away, then the kitchen was full of warm, friendly steam that swirled in the air and made the window look like it was crying its eyes out. It seemed to me the kitchen was full of steam a lot of the time. My mam always seemed to be making steam. If it wasn't steam from the bubbling laundry water, it was steam from a kettle on to do the dishes or to make tea. Because she was for ever making tea, my mam was. She'd have just made a pot of tea or be just about to make a pot of tea or have the kettle on low, trickling tiny wisps of steam, ready in case anyone should all of a sudden want a pot of tea. Even when nothing was bubbling away on the stove, cigarette smoke would be puffing out of her mouth like steam. As far as I knew, my mam had invented steam. When I asked my dad about that, he said, "No, but if we could only sell the steam she does make, boys-o-boys but we'd be on the pig's back, what?"

You couldn't always depend on the steam to come when it was supposed to, though. Something about a watched pot that made no sense to me at all. Wouldn't a pot boil whether you were watching it or not? How would it know you were watching it? There had to be another reason. It turned out there was. I heard my mam complaining about the spuds not being done yet. "The divil's in that pot, so he is," she said, putting the lid back. So that was it: the pot was haunted. Now that made more sense than not boiling because it didn't like you looking at it.

When I had the kitchen to myself, I whispered to the steaming pot, "Are you in there, devil?" Inside the pot the devil burped, and I thought I'd take a look at him. Just an inch, that was all I lifted the heavy lid, but the devil saw his chance and rushed out in a scalding whoosh that made me scream and drop the lid. Now what would I do? I looked all over but couldn't find the escaped devil. I didn't like the idea of him wandering the house and maybe dragging us off to hell, one by one, but if that was his game, he wasn't going to get me. I put the lid back and said nothing, just scrammed out to the canal bank with my fishing net and jam jar.

It turned out I was worrying over nothing, because everything was fine and the crisis was over by teatime with the devil back on the job. "The divil's in that kettle, so he is," said my mam to my dad, who was waiting for his tea. Sure enough, I could hear him knocking to get out, but I wasn't going to fall for that again. "You just stay there, you little, black enamel, horned bugger," I whispered down the spout, and the thwarted devil hissed angrily back.

I felt that maybe I could do with the devil now, though. Have him drag some of the people in this house off to hell out of it and let me have my windowsill back. Because by this time I'd lost the use of that perfect parade ground to line up lead soldiers ready to attack at first light. Lost it to a baby who didn't even know what lead soldiers were. When it got too big for the cot, my mam would put the most recent baby between me and the windowsill. "It's for protection," I was told. "So the baby won't roll out of the bed." What harm if it did roll out? It wouldn't get lost, would it? It'd only be under the bed.

It looked like it might be a long time before I got the window back, because my mam seemed to be picking up babies now like they were stray cats. The bedroom floor began to disappear as iron-framed beds of various sizes were added one by one until finally the whole room was full of beds so close to each other that a jiggle on one set them all quivering like noisy jelly. There was even a small bed in the corner that had no floor access at all, and whoever was in that one had to crawl over another bed to get to the small area of lino that was left clear.

At the head of the bed I shared with the latest roll-away was an alcove which the bedhead didn't quite fit into, so there was a gap. Sometimes I would escape over the top and slither down the wall into the darkness below and hide. Just watch out for the pot. Depending on who had used it last, it could be under any of the beds – and it might be full. For safety's sake, it was best not to move until your eyes got used to the dark. When they did, you were in a forest of bed legs where iron trees came together overhead in a canopy of saggy springs and mattresses that sometimes bulged alarmingly. This forest floor was always worth exploring, because once I found a penny. But the owners of pockets full of pennies must have been awfully vigilant, because I never found more than that one penny. Either that or there were other scavengers scouring the forest floor. Another drawback to no longer being an only.

12

"**F**ISHES DON'T HAVE jayzis ears," Jacko said. With our fishing nets and jam jars, we were searching for pinkeens in the shallow water at the canal's edge. Ears or not, something had startled them. Dozens of the little fishes, like silver paint flicked from the end of a brush, were darting for the cover of the reeds.

"Explain it to me so," I said, turning my net inside out to clear out the bits of moss that I'd picked while trawling for pinkeens. "How do they know the barge is coming if they can't hear it? Is it because it comes at the same time every day, then? Is that it?"

"No! Fishes don't have jayzis watches, either. It must be somethin' else. Lookout fish, or somethin'."

Down among the reeds at the water's edge, we had been too low, but when we climbed back on to the path, sure enough we could see a canal barge in the distance and faintly hear the far-off chug-chug of its engine as it made its way from the heart of Ireland to the Grand Canal Docks in Ringsend. However they did it, the pinkeens always seemed to know before we did that a barge was on its way. Bermo said it wasn't the barge at all but Jacko slipping and sliding along the bank and dropping his fishing net into the water every minute that frightened them.

"That's a lotta bollix," said Jacko, slipping and dropping his fishing net into the water.

The fishing net was a pocket of white gauzy stuff on a wire frame fixed to the end of a bamboo pole. Nor were they cheap, those nets; sixpence each they cost. Mr Lynch had them arranged in a barrel in the corner of his shop, like a display of huge white blooms. Jacko's net didn't come from Lynch's, though. After Jacko having broken so many, his dad wanted to know did he think he was made of money or what, that he could be buying fishing nets for him every day of the week. Jacko's fishing net was the sturdy handle of a sweeping brush with one of his mam's old nylon stockings fixed to it on a hoop of galvanised wire.

When a pinkeen was nabbed, he was put into a jam jar full of water that had a string tied around the neck as a handle. So the fish would feel at home, a sup of moss might be thrown in along with a few pebbles, and a bit of bread so he wouldn't go hungry. If he was thirsty, sure hadn't he the whole jar full of water?

Me and Bermo usually managed to nab at least a few pinkeens: Jacko was a whole different ball of wax altogether. He rarely caught any pinkeens at all, and those he did manage to catch had a fifty-fifty chance of escape depending on where he dropped his jar, because he was bound to drop it somewhere before the day was out. If he dropped it into the canal, the fish swam out to freedom. If he dropped it on the footpath, hard cheese. He'd rush around trying to pick them up, but chances were he'd slip on one little wriggler and sit down on the others and mash them flat. And all this rushing around, of course, greatly increased the chances of him doing a header into the canal.

The trouble with Jacko, you see, was that he was so excitable he'd lose the managing of himself entirely sometimes. In his eagerness, he'd reach in too far with his net and would topple forward – both arms flailing like he was trying to fly – as he did a slow-motion belly flopper into the water. Or he'd pick a close-in pinkeen and get in under it all right, but then he'd jerk up so fast with the net that he'd spin himself into the canal like a top. The first few times he fell in, it was panic stations, but we soon learned to be relaxed about it. Bermo, sounding real bored, would say, "Don't tell me Jacko's after falling into the jayzis canal again." With a yawn, I'd reply, "Yes, Bermo, he jayzis has."

13

FROM WHERE IT started at the River Liffey in Ringsend, the Grand Canal stretched for miles deep into the country. My granda said there were rumours it had been seen as far west as Tullamore, but you couldn't always believe my granda, who was given to *raiméis-ing* sometimes. But, however far it went, canal barges used it in a daily delivery of goods to and from far-flung towns. The barge going into the country might have big barrels of porter for the countrymen in it, which it would swap for potatoes or something to bring back to Dublin. And they held a lot, those barges. A full one moved slowly, its deck just inches above the water. When empty, it rode so high that the man at the back working the rudder would have to duck going under the bridges.

The oncoming barge pushed a big wave in front of it that rushed up the canal bank, flattening the reeds, swamping the path and churning the water a muddy brown. This spoiled our fishing, but it gave us another game: dodge-the-wave. The trick was to wait till the last minute before jumping out of the way of this furious water, and whoever jumped last was the winner. Of course, it wasn't really much of a contest if Jacko was along. He was usually so soaked by this time that another dollop of water didn't worry him.

I wondered how the pinkeens fared in the muddy water. Could they see in it or was it like a sandstorm in the desert to them? Jacko thought that maybe they had seeing-eye dogfish or something to lead them around till the water cleared. Anyway, until it did clear, we couldn't get back to our fishing, but the barge drivers were always good for a laugh. Sometimes they were even better than the fishing. "Hey, mister," I called one day. "Will you bring us back a parrot?"

"Do you know what?" he called back. "I had one for you. But the crocodile I got for someone else ate it."

Some of them didn't even wait to be shouted at but started the ball rolling themselves. Over the thud-thud of his engine, the man at the rudder called out to us on the bank, "How's the fishing, men?" He waved a large, bent, smoke-billowing pipe in the air.

"Oh, deadly, mister." Fishing nets flapping above our heads like it was butterflies we were after – or maybe flying fish – we ran along the bank beside the barge. "Jacko's just after bein' pulled in by an octopus. That's why he's all wet."

"Be the hokey! Is that a fact? An octopus? Do you know what I'm going to tell you? That's not something you see every day on the canal. I'd have him stuffed, so I would."

"Ha! We were only codding you, mister." Shouting louder, and running slower because we were getting short of breath and falling behind: "There's no octopus; Jacko just fell in by himself. Like he does nearly every day." Stopped now, we were holding our sides and puffing as the barge went on. The bargeman called back through cupped hands, "It's your friend Jacko I'm talking about. It's him I'd have stuffed. Sounds like a right caution altogether."

When a barge came to a lock, the lock-keeper came out of his cottage, waving a big handle like a rattle and, depending on which way the barge was going, would either close or open the big gates to raise or lower the water. Raising the water was more exciting. When the barge was in the lock, the keeper would close the gates behind it and then wind open the shutters in the gates on the high-water side to let the water come splashing and gushing in through the openings like Niagara. The driver would have to skip away to the other end of the barge to keep himself dry. And if the barge was empty, it was so light it lurched and swayed and banged against the walls of the lock as the flooding water swirled and foamed around it. Only for the tyres hanging from its sides, it would have been battered to bits as the rising water brought it up to the level of the rest of the canal.

My Uncle Bill told me a story of how a coach and horses had fallen into a lock in the old days because of fog or ice or something. Or maybe some oul' fella had spat a gollier on to the road and one of the horses slipped on it. Anyway, the lock-keeper came out sprightly enough with his big handle. "Don't worry," says he. "I'll float yez out," says he. And didn't he open the shutters to let the water in and drown the lot of them.

14

ONE THING BROUGHT back from the country in the vast holds of the barges was turf. Covered in tarpaulin, mounds of it rose up almost as high as the rudder-man's head. Each load was added to a huge, growing pile of the stuff down on the docks: turf for all the fireplaces in the city of Dublin. I thought it would be a good idea if they were to shovel it on to the canal bank as they passed and let everyone gather their own. That way at least some of us would get some. Not like last winter when there was no turf. Or there was plenty of turf, but nobody got any.

"The docks piled high with turf and coal that nobody can get at because it's frozen into a solid lump," my dad said. "You'd need dynamite to shift it. And we're freezing here for want of something to burn. The idiots."

It got so cold that winter the canal froze over and you could walk on the water like Our Lord. I went with my dad to examine it. And Bermo with his dad. And everyone else with their dads, because all the dads were off work on account of the frost had shut everything down. Everyone except Jacko, that is. His mam and dad were so terrified at the mischief he'd maybe get up to under these strange conditions that he was confined to barracks until the thaw came. The odd time he got out, it was under escort, and even then he wasn't let anywhere near the canal. He'd be seen going by on the house side of the road, his dad on the outside, holding tight to his collar for fear he'd make a run for it, crash through the ice and never be heard from again.

In their coats and hats and scarves, the dads stood on the canal bank, smoking and nodding and saying, "Did you ever see anything like it?" Someone said, yes, he had; the year he was married was a worse winter. Another someone said, "Don't be talkin'; there's a permanent frost in my house ever since I got married."

After a lot of pleading with my dad, and promising not to tell my mam, I got to walk out a little bit through the reeds. Unwinding my scarf, I held one end of it and he held the other, and slowly, one sliding foot in front of the other, I walked where I never dreamed I'd walk, on the slippery, silver surface of the Grand Canal.

Even some of the men tested the ice with cautious feet like they were walking on eggs. There was the sound of cracking when Bermo's dad got out a bit, and everyone let a roar out of them and skidded, laughing, for the bank. There, in safety and wonder, they stood in the weak sunlight, blowing on their fingers and slapping their arms around themselves, steamy breath mixed with cigarette smoke billowing from their mouths, the thrown-away fag-ends bouncing off the ice in showers of sparks instead of going out with a fizz. I wondered if it was frozen all the way to the bottom. And if so, could I chip out a pinkeen or two to bring to Jacko?

The men agreed the canal was an extraordinary sight all right. And how still and quiet everything seemed. And how Mother Nature could shut down a whole city when she took it into her head to show off her bag of tricks. And wasn't the cold at night something fierce altogether? And did anybody know where there was a bit of coal or a bit of wood to be got at all? One of the men said there'd be no guests staying in his house ever again because he'd burned the spare bed to get a bit of heat. "The headboard goes tonight," he said. "And that's the last of it. It gave us a fair bit o' heat out of it while it was in it. And d'y'know what? The missus used to complain it was a very cold bed."

Someone else said, "At least it's warm down in the boozer, wat? Thanks b't'Jayzis, wat?" All agreed it was a terrible thing indeed that a man had to go to a pub to get a bit of heat and they laughed and said they'd see each other there later, so they would.

15

I TRIED TO DROWN myself in the canal one time – if the woman who brought me home to my mam sopping wet was to be believed.

"I seen him, missus," she said. "He wandered up under the bridge there at Harold's Cross, to where it was good and deep. No reeds nor nothing, just a straight drop and, God between us and all harm, in he went, plop." The other women behind her were bobbing their heads and clucking in sympathy.

Stripping the clothes off me, my mam scrubbed so hard with the towel that I felt raw. "Oh, dear God in heaven," she said. "Why? Why did you do such a thing?" Even if I'd tried to answer, I wouldn't have been able to, because between the scrubbing and the cold, I was shaking so much my teeth were going like a Spanish dancer's clickers.

"Ah, sure, maybe it was an accident," said another woman.

"No! Definny." This was the first woman again. "I seen him pick the deep spot and jump in. It was no accident. He was trying to off himself, the poor little beggar. Whatever's weighin' on his mind." She gave my mam a funny sideways look.

Another woman said, ah no, she knew the family and there was nothing to be suspicious about as we were all good-living Christians, thanks be t'God an' his holy mother. The first one said that, oh well, she knew what she'd seen, that's all. "An' lucky there was a man cycling past who jumped off of his bike at me scream, grabbed the youngster b'the collar when he came up splutterin' and hauled him on to the bank in a flash."

The woman who knew we were all good-living Christians had taken me by one hand, the woman who knew what she'd seen had taken the other, and between them I squelched homeward, sockless feet slithery and slimy inside wet sandals. The crowd of women and children following us along the street got larger with each

splashy step; what had started out with just a couple of the concerned was a cavalcade of the curious by the time it got to the house. Everybody clumped around the door, frankly waiting to see if the excitement was over yet or not. My mam thanked them all and said firmly that I was going to be fine as soon as she got me dried off and, "Excuse me now," she said as she swung the door closed.

Before it closed all the way, I heard the first woman say to her convoy, "Jayzis. Did you see the poor little beggar in his pelt? Sure lookit, I often seen more meat on an X-a-ray." My mam gave the door an extra push that made it close with a bang.

Putting a match to the fire, she asked hopefully, "Did you trip, or what?" I shook my head, watching goose-pimpled knees, like sucked gobstoppers, go through the spectrum from orangey-purple back to their more usual pink. "You jumped in then?" I nodded. "On purpose?" I nodded again. "Oh, holy father! Why? In God's name, why?"

It had made perfect sense at the time. But now that I was being questioned, I felt the logic slipping away. There didn't seem to be any point in trying to explain that I just wanted to walk around down there among the fishes and the reeds; that I wanted to see what the fishes' world looked like; that I wanted to saunter out to the middle where it was real deep and see what I could find in the mud.

The thing was, I hadn't expected to get wet at all. This was before Jacko had started demonstrating over and over that water was indeed wet and went all the way to the bottom. What I'd thought was, that what I could see, the top, was all there was to it; just that thin, wet skin like a sheet of liquid glass. If I could get past the top fast enough, I figured, I'd hardly get wet at all; no more than from a summer shower. That was why I'd needed the deep water, so that I could get through the thin skin quickly without lingering at the surface where the damp was.

The fire was coming along nicely now, and I was comfortably warm in the big towel, and the whole thing was too complicated to explain. "I seen a big reddy-gold roach swimmin' under the bridge and I wanted to catch it," I said. If this wasn't the truth, neither was it a complete lie. Seeing the roach had made me want to look at things from its point of view; to find out was it made of real gold; and was that why you never saw roaches near the water's edge where they might be caught in your net, because they were so valuable? Maybe two-and-sixpence an ounce.

My mam seemed satisfied enough with this explanation because she didn't keep going on about it, just told me to stay away from the deep water under the bridge and to stick to the pinkeens in the future. She didn't have to tell me. I wouldn't be trying that experiment again. But even though I'd learned something that was probably useful, I was a little disappointed as well. It was as thought the canal had somehow let itself down, had lied to me, had made itself out to be something grander than it really was. In actual fact, there was nothing special about it at all. It was just like the plain, ordinary, common-or-garden tap water we had in the scullery.

16

WHEN THE CANAL got so silted up that the barges were scraping the bottom, it was time to call the dredger in. This dredger, loud with clanking chains and cables and shouting dredger-men, was a special barge fitted with a crane and big-toothed jaws that hauled up cascading scoopfuls of runny brown mud from the canal bottom. This mud was then dropped on the bank where it spread out over the reeds and the path. And there was much interesting stuff in that mud: old bike frames, bed springs, kettles, wheels, tin cans, prams, everything you could think of, all of it rusty and slimy with canal snails. A bike wheel with no spokes made a great hoop that you could beat up and down the road with a stick. Pram wheels were prized. Four of them with their tyres and you could build a go-car. Much better than the little ball-bearing wheels you might find in the Ever Ready dump, the pram wheels gave you speed and silence that the ball-bearings didn't. You could whiz up behind a woman so fast that she wouldn't hear you coming and, at the very least, was bound to let a scream out of her; with a bit of luck she might even drop her shopping all over the footpath. An old car tyre was almost as good as the whole car. Scrunched up inside it, you could have your pals wheel you along the road. If you could trust them not to point you in the direction of the canal, that is, because you'd be so dizzy from turning over and over that you wouldn't have a clue where you were going. When you got on your feet again, you spun for a few minutes on your own private axis, your balance banjaxed and bockety.

But whatever it was that was dredged up from the bottom of the canal, the Portobello Road rules of salvage applied to it: first to pull the article from the streaming mud could claim it as his own. Jacko saw something interesting sticking out of the jaws of the scoop one day and was so excited that he was almost buried in muck when the jaws opened. Then he nearly sliced the fingers off himself in his eagerness as he whipped the article he had his eye on from the runny mess. It was a soldier's bayonet.

"One of our brave lads must have thrown that away while on the run from the English," my dad said with pride in his voice when he heard of the find.

"Or maybe it was on the run to Flanagan's Bar for last call he was, and he threw it away in the interests of speed," said my granda, who didn't always agree with my dad about the Irish and the English. Although he was so old now that he was retired from work as a lighthouse keeper, he still rode his bike, sometimes cycling all the way over from Donnycarney for a visit.

Granda smoked a pipe the whole time, and his clothes always smelt tobacco-y; he claimed his waistcoat was that saturated with tobacco, he could smoke it if he was stuck. His dark blue light-keeper's coat with the brass buttons gave him the look of a sea captain. Up close, you could see that each button had a picture on it of a lighthouse flashing its light out over the ocean to guide the sailors home. And I could hear his heart go tic-tic-tic through the blue coat. It was his watch really, but when I was little, my granda used to pretend it was his heart and would take it out and wind it up. "Got to keep it wound," he'd say. "If I ever forget to wind it, I'm a goner, so I am." He'd smack his lips, blow on his tea and drink it from the saucer with a slurp.

Spread among the pockets of his waistcoat were what he called his four Ps: pipe, penknife, pouch and plug tobacco. The flakes cut from the plug were ground between his palms and teased out into slivers that he stuffed into the pipe. Then, with great sucking draws that made his cheeks go hollow and the match flame disappear down into the bowl of the pipe, the tobacco was lit. A little silver lid with holes in it for the smoke to escape was placed on the bowl, and he puffed away until he was engulfed in a cloud of smoke and any tobacco smell that might have been blown off his coat on the cycle over was replaced and everything was back to normal. When I asked why he put the lid on the pipe, he said it was to keep his dottle dry for Grandma. "Hates a wet dottle, she does." The way he laughed, I knew it was a private joke of his own and I'd get no more sense out of him on that subject. He joked a lot, my

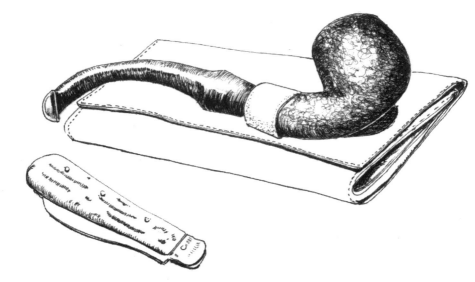

granda did. He'd sometimes say – if nobody else was around, "Here, pull that," and make his bum bark by having me pull on his finger.

My dad was sure about the bayonet, but my granda had been all over and seen everything and wasn't inclined to be impressed with a rusty bayonet that might or might not have been used in what might or might not have been the fight for Ireland's freedom. But my dad was sure. A great one for the honour and glory of Ireland, my dad was. Listening to him talk about the wonderful literature there was in the Irish language made me want to learn to speak it. I used to dream of the honour it would be to fight against the English if I had to. My dad told me about all the brave men who had died for Ireland: Robert Emmet, O'Donovan Rossa, Wolfe Tone, Pádraig Pearse. And he could sing songs about all of them that would break your heart. "Only a boy, Robert Emmet was when he was hanged, drawn and quartered by the English," he said. "They captured him out in Rathfarnham at Sarah Curran's house. Yes, they knew he'd come to see his true love, and like the low curs they were, they hid and waited. So he was captured for love of a woman and he died for love of his country. The English! Don't talk to me about the English. Didn't we have a civilisation, a culture and laws of our own when the Britons were still wearing wolf skins, painting themselves blue and living in caves?"

I couldn't think of a higher calling than to fight for Ireland and swore I would, too, if I had to. Not that there was much chance of that now. Hadn't the Irish driven the English off the soil of Ireland and weren't they free at last? But my granda didn't seem to think the Irish rulers were much better. "English rulers or Irish rulers, same difference. Doesn't matter a damn who's in power, you and me still has to break stones. They're only out for themselves, them politicians."

One night after my dad, with tears in his eyes, had just finished singing about Roddy McCorley going to die on the bridge of Toome today, my granda said, "Dying for your country is all very well. But living for it is a darn sight harder, sometimes. And I'm not talking about these clowns that everyone voted for because they swore they'd done their bit for Ireland in 1916. They're not living for their country, that lot. They're living *off* their country. Sure lookit, if even half of those that swore they were in the General Post Office on Easter Monday really had been there, there would have been no need at all for the English to bring gunboats up the Liffey to bombard the place. It would have burst at the seams of its own accord from overcrowding."

"Well, what about afterward?" My dad wanted to know. "The English putting them up against the wall like traitors. And James Connolly so badly wounded he couldn't even stand. Brought to his death in an ambulance he was, and shot in a chair. What about that, then?"

"You're right. That was a mistake, making martyrs out of them. They should have just given them a boot up the arse and sent them home. That would have been the end of it."

"But they couldn't do that, could they? Savages."

"But not a patch on us when we got going though, eh?" My granda was getting red and grinding tobacco fiercely in his palms as he spoke. "They only executed a handful. When we got the Free State under way and had our own little civil war, we executed hundreds out in the yard at Kilmainham Jail. Hundreds! Of our own!"

My dad hesitated, then did a thing with his hands like he was shooing away flies, as if to say, that wasn't what we were talking about. The outstretched finger of one hand hammered in rhythm with his speech as he said, "The men of 1916. They weren't English traitors, they were Irish heroes. And what about Roger Casement? Shot as an English traitor, and him Irish."

"You'll be telling me next that Lord Haw Haw wasn't a traitor," said my granda, ferociously teasing the ground tobacco out into strands with his fingers.

"Well, if it comes to that. . ." My dad was getting red in the face himself. "No, he wasn't a traitor. Whatever else Lord Haw Haw was – and he was a bad article right enough – he wasn't a traitor. Because he wasn't an Englishman. William Joyce was no Englishman."

I thought Lord Haw Haw was a funny name and wondered if he was one of the clowns my granda had been talking about that everyone voted for. But when they got talking about how Lord

Haw Haw had been hanged, I was shocked. Why would they hang a clown? Was he not funny enough for them? Even so, hanging him, that was taking it a bit far. I imagined a big-footed, red-nosed, sad-eyed clown hanging by his neck from a lamp-post just because he couldn't make the king and queen of England laugh.

17

"THERE'S MORE THAN one way of killing a cat than choking it with the best creamery butter." That was one of my mam's sayings. Well, I didn't know anything about that, but I did know there was more than one way of getting on a bike, so there was, and it was a great morning's entertainment watching the men of Portobello Road set about it in their different ways. Some would scoot along, one foot on the pedal, and then throw the leg over. Some would throw the leg over from a standing start. Some got on from one side of the bike, some from the other. Some ran with it and jumped on to the saddle without touching the pedal at all. One of the younger men would sometimes push his bike forward and jump into the saddle from behind, and that was kind of showy, I thought. Except my dad said that for some reason that way wasn't recommended; something about starting a family. As far as I could see, it only a bike the man was starting.

But Jacko's dad's way of getting on his bike really took the biscuit altogether. He began by scooting along in the normal way, but then, instead of throwing the free leg over the back wheel like everyone else, he'd bring it up in front of himself and over the crossbar before sitting back in the saddle. When I asked why he did that, my dad said vaguely, "Oh, bit of trouble in the groin area." I didn't know what part of the bike that was, but I thought he should get it fixed soon because he looked a right eejit getting on like that.

Bermo's dad was usually the first one out in the morning. He was a boiler man and, as he said, had to "have the system steamin' away, firin' on all cylinders before the big nobs get to their offices, or be-the-hokey there'd be ructions".

In dribs and drabs then, the others would come wheeling out of their hallways. Propped up by a pedal against the edge of the footpath, the bike became a footrest for the putting on of the cycle clips. The men good morning-ed each other and lit up the day's first cigarette – or maybe the second if they'd been down the yard to the lav. Hands would be clapped and rubbed together briskly as though to press into existence a brilliant diamond of a day from the thin mist of the morning. Then the cloth cap would go on the head, well pulled down against the breeze. A hand would be passed over the front of the trousers, checking fly-buttons, followed by a pat at the side pocket – yes, brown-papered sandwich in place. Maybe the lapel would be lifted away from the chest to check that any letters they had been given that morning to post were in the inside pocket – or that the ones they'd forgotten to post yesterday were still there.

Sometimes a bunch of the men would rush out at the same time, and that was something to see, especially if they were a bit late, because then everyone got in everyone else's way. It was like a massed start at the Tour de France, pushed bikes getting tangled, hurried leaps into saddles, barked shins, near collisions, the lot. Except it didn't have the colour, of course. Bright colours might be all right in France, where they drank red wine outdoors, wearing yellow berets under the hot sun, but it wouldn't do in Ireland where they drank black pints indoors in dark cloth caps. A coloured bike, if you could get one, would be thought frivolous. These were hard-working, serious bikes, and they were a hard-working, serious colour – black. Hercules, BSA, Raleigh, Rudge; no matter who the manufacturer was, he made the working man's bike black.

And then there was Mr Smith, who worked to a strict timetable of his own. No matter what flurry was going on around him, Mr Smith wouldn't pull away from the curb before his time. On our road, we had God's time, daylight saving time and Smith's time. Consulting the big pocket watch from his bulging waistcoat, he counted off the last few seconds like he was a train on a timetable. All set. Off we go. Left foot on the left pedal. Scoot with the right foot. One, two, three, over the back wheel with the leg and into the saddle; a few quick pedals to get the bike up to speed, then he'd sit back drawing on his pipe, plumes of smoke billowing behind him like he really was a steam engine.

Then it was the schoolboys' turn. Never as friendly as the men, these big boys always seemed a bit worried and frantic and scarcely said a word to each other. Heads down, schoolbags clamped to the back carriers or hanging down from the crossbars, they pedalled, stern-faced, to school.

Finally – the departure of the dads and scurry of the schoolboys over – it was time for my dad to go to work. This was when he had the shoe-repair shop out in Inchicore and could go in whenever he wanted. He liked the day well aired, he said, before going out in it, so he went in a bit later in the mornings and would stay a bit later in the evenings – if necessary. I thought it was great that my dad worked for himself, because when things were slow at his work, we would sometimes go off together on his bike. My mam didn't seem too pleased about these jaunts for some reason. Maybe, she said, if things were organised better at work, there'd be no time for gallivanting. I thought things were organised perfectly; how many boys could go off with their dad on his bike in the middle of the week?

He'd made a small saddle for me that was attached to the crossbar. A crosspiece was attached to the downbar for my feet. Legs astride the crossbar and with my hands between his on the handlebar, it was like I was riding my own bike. On these jaunts, we'd usually go somewhere far, somewhere where there was only country and no houses for miles. Tallaght maybe. Or Old Bawn. Our picnic in a biscuit tin tied to the back carrier, my dad would cycle until he found a nice spot, and then we'd sit and he'd tell stories about Diarmaid and Gráinne, or Fionn Mac Cumhaill, or Oisín in Tir na nÓg, or the Children of Lir, or Cúchulainn, or the kings of Tara. I was always a little disappointed when I opened my eyes after one of these stories to find we were still in modern times with bikes and steam engines, instead of back in the old days with heroes on horses.

Mind you, there were heroes in these times, too. Or at least famous people. Mickser Reid was one. He was a little man with a huge head nearly as big as the rest of him who was known all over the city. Everywhere he went, people called out to him, "How's it goin', Mickser?" And, "Good to see ya, Mickser." And, "Hope ye're keepin' well, Mickser." You'd think he was a film star.

Bang-Bang from Inchicore was another who was well known. Swinging on the bar out the back door of the buses, he'd shoot at any suspicious-looking pedestrians with a big key he held like a gun in his hand. "Bang, bang," he'd say as he riddled you with his key. "Bang, bang." And of course, if he got you in his sights, you had to play the game and grab yourself like you were shot. Bang-Bang came into my dad's shoe shop one time. In he ran, twirling his key on his trigger finger. Taking aim, he shot my dad, bang! Blowing the smoke away from the end of the key, he then shot me, bang! Out the door and up to the corner he ran, key cocked and at the ready, and he jumped on to a passing bus. Bang! Bang! Any pursuers were taken care of with that last volley. My dad said that was something not everyone could boast of; that being shot by Bang-Bang made me a true Dubliner.

18

W ITH THE EARLY morning bustle out of the way, Portobello Road quietened down until the mams came out about their business a little later and livened it up again. There were the letter boxes and doorknobs and house numbers to be polished with Brasso; or the windows to be cleaned with vinegar and newspaper; or, at some of the houses, red-geranium-filled window boxes to be taken care of; or perhaps the front step had to be scrubbed while the mams talked. I was never sure if they talked because they were scrubbing or scrubbed so they could talk, but whether it was planned in advance or not, as soon as one basin of soapy water appeared, several more sploshed on to steps in the immediate vicinity within minutes. Then, when they were finished, they all gathered around the last step and waited for them to dry. I enjoyed when it was our doorstep the mothers came to, and I'd keep quiet behind the front door and listen. I didn't always know what they were on about, but some things you knew were important the way the voices lowered and the speaker's head would turn to give a quick check in both directions to make sure the object of the conversation wasn't on the horizon. I'd listen to the men, too, whenever I could, and whatever the differences between the conversations, one thing was exactly the same: that was what both parties did when they realised you were listening. Then they'd switch to a sort of code of nods and winks and spelling-out of words in a bid to throw you off the scent.

"I wonder what the men do be talkin' about among themselves when we're not there," one of the women said one time.

My mam said, "Probably the same things we talk about."

Bermo's mam said, "Why, the dirty beasts." And the mothers on the steps laughed, and the cigarette packets were passed around again. I could never understand why step mothers in fairy tales were always supposed to be wicked. The mothers on these steps

BOCKETY 79

were a panic altogether. And they were well able for the hucksters that called some afternoons with their bags and boxes full of things they swore no woman could live without. When it turned out the women actually could live without them, these men would turn to more everyday things like floor polish or shoe polish, and once somebody tried to sell silver polish. "Is it silver polish?" the women wanted to know. "Jayzis, mister, you really are in the wrong street this time. Silver, how are ya!"

One time when I was alone, there was a knock at the door. A tinker stood there asking had we any umbrellas he could fix like new for us. "All these umbrellas I have here under me oxter," he pointed to the bundle under his arm, the two eyes of him darting about the hallway behind me, "I got up and down the street. Sure, I'm well known in these parts. Aye! And well trusted too. Or they wouldn't ha' give me these to fix, would they? I can put in new ribs, new handles, new cover if you like. Show us that one behind ya there in the hallstand."

I handed over the umbrella my mam had got just before Christmas and the tinker examined it carefully, opening it and closing it and twirling it. "This is a nice brolly all right, and it would be worth fixing up, so it would. See that tear, sure the rain must come bucketin' in through that." But the umbrella was closed again before I got a chance to see. "And you needn't pay me now," he rushed on. "I'll be back with the job done on Tuesda', how's that? Couldn't be fairer than that, what?"

When my mam came in, she was very annoyed. "Well," she said. "That's the last time that brolly will keep the rain off a perm of mine." And when I found the bundle of old umbrellas thrown away in the reeds along the canal that afternoon, I realised she was right. I'd been had. The tinker had been on the mooch for new umbrellas he could sell, and the old ones were just a decoy. "A sprat," as my mam said in another of her sayings, "to catch a mackerel."

Sometimes it was a tinker woman would come along begging at the doors, always with a baby wrapped in a shawl, and the baby was always supposed to be starving. "Starving, my eye," my dad said, making a jeer of my mam for being so soft. "Did you get a good look at that baby? It's the same baby that was here last week with a different mother." Or they'd ask for a cup of milk or water maybe. "Only" – my dad again – "to get you out of the hall so that they could root through the hallstand. That's probably where my bicycle clips and lamp went."

My mam gave a little sniff – she didn't like being made a jeer of. "Or maybe you left them down in Clarke's one night you were so happy, and one of your cronies liberated them for you." Clarke's was where my dad sometimes went for cigarettes. Now he was the one was miffed, and he stamped out in a huff, banging the back door behind him as he went down the yard to the lav with the *Irish Press*, his packet of Sweet Afton and his thoughts.

19

"ST BLAISE IS the man you want, missus," said Bermo's mam. The women on the street were having yet another confab about Jacko. Sometimes they'd gather and talk of his latest disasters like he was an ongoing serial at the picture house. *Jacko the Jinxed, A Dublin Tragedy in Umpteen Episodes.* And Jacko's frazzled-looking mam would say he had her heart scalded, so he had. Cures would be discussed and tried and always failed. The mams always ended up saying in the sort of voice you could imagine them using if they were trying to convince someone who had lost a leg that it might grow back, "Please God now, he'll grow out of it." They'd been saying that for a long time.

Actually, I felt there was a certain security about having Jacko around, because if trouble was mooching about looking for a place to squat, it'd be Jacko it would squat on, not you. He was a sort of lightning conductor for trouble. Sure, you could be working away with your dad's hammers and nails and saws all day, building a fort or something, without doing a bit of damage; Jacko had only to reach for the butter to send everything on the table clattering to the floor in smithereens.

And now it was St Blaise's turn to take part in the latest instalment of the ongoing quest to cure Jacko. Bermo's mam went on, "Sure lookit, one time I had a throat on me that was like sandpaper and a voice that was a croak would have done a bullfrog proud, but St Blaise fixed me up. They have a relic or something in that church on the Quays."

"Oh, yes, nothing like a rub of the relic," says one of the women, and all the others started coughing and spluttering as cigarette smoke went the wrong way.

Bermo's mam went on. "Anyways, they have two blessed candles tied into the shape of a cross and they tucked them under me chin and said a holy prayer. Next thing wasn't I out on the Ha'penny Bridge and me singing like a thrush."

"Sure you didn't pop into the snug first?" asked Mrs Synott.

"Oh, now, you may jeer if you want, but I'm tellin' you I was better." Then her eyes twinkled. "And, yes, if you must know, I did have a wee drop of Three Swallow in the Irish House after. But it was only to celebrate being cured, so it was." So the women were convinced. It was agreed that if anyone could do anything for Jacko, it was your man, St Blaise. St Blaise was really supposed to be only for throats, but wasn't it worth a try? They figured that if Jacko's hands could only be got to stop breaking things, surely the rest of him would fall into line.

When St Blaise's feast day came round, a procession of prams, women and children set off for the church on the Quays to get Jacko's hands blessed. Down the canal past Bloomfield Avenue and along Windsor Terrace went the line of prams, like a wagon train into the Old West. Scouts with hurley-stick rifles kept a sharp eye out for Injins who might attack as we turned down Clanbrassil Street and headed towards the badlands of the Coombe.

It turned out to be more of a hike to the church than we thought; not even at Patrick Street yet, and already we were a jaded bunch of little cowboys indeed. Most of us had already cached our wooden weapons, which had become progressively heavier, in various prams. It's not much farther now, the mams kept telling us, but they were looking a bit bunched themselves by the time we'd crossed under the arch of Christ Church on to the slope of Winetavern Street and the last leg of the journey. Some of the boys who had started off full of beans and running all over the place were now scrunched up, banjaxed, at the foot of their baby brothers' and sisters' prams. And with the added weight, the mams were having a bit of a struggle keeping these prams from running away from them down the steep hill and were leaning back at alarming angles as counterbalance. If a pram was to get loose, there'd be nothing to stop it until it hit the quay wall at the bottom of the hill, which would probably catapult the occupants into the River Liffey and drown them – if the crash hadn't already killed them. But, fair play to the mams, they made it all the way down to Merchant's Quay without losing a single pram.

As their hands dipped into the holy water font, some of the

women turned longing eyes across the road in the direction of the Irish House. Maybe on the way home, the eyes said. Heads nodded in agreement at the unspoken suggestion, and sprinkling themselves with holy water, they traipsed into the holy gloom.

Jacko was one of those who had finished the journey asleep at the foot of his sister's pram – the main performer and him passed out cold. Didn't matter; he was lifted out and frog-marched up the church, half-asleep. At the altar rail, his mam grabbed his wrists and held his hands out, one over the other, for the priest with the candles. These candles were crossed over each other in an X, like the bones on a pirate's flag. Jacko's startled eyes opened wide. Who knows what thoughts went through his mind at that moment? Perhaps to his sleep-befuddled brain, things coming down toward him recalled the time when he was nearly guillotined by the broken window pane in my house. Anyway, whatever it was got into him, didn't he let a yelp out of him and fling his hands upward. The blessed candles went flying into the air, crossbones that would find a skull in a minute. The priest took a startled step back, bumped into the altar boy behind him, and they both went staggering backward, trying to catch up to themselves. When the altar boy hit the steps, it was game over. Down he went, legs in the air, skirts flying. There was a sound from him like a rubber ball bursting as the priest – the big, fat, heavy priest – landed on top of him.

Jacko's mam collapsed like a whimpering rag doll across the altar rail. "Oh, dear, sweet, merciful God in heaven," she moaned. "What did I ever do to deserve being lumbered with such a gallumping lump of a bull in a china shop like that?"

Bermo's mam grabbed her by the arm. "C'mon," she said. "Let's get t'hell out of here before we're all excommuni-bloody-cated."

Jacko's mam grabbed him by the ear and dragged him down the aisle. "B'Jayzis," she prayed fervently at the door. "Let me not go one step beyond the snug across the road for at least another hour."

"Come with me," said my mam as she took me by the hand. She led me away as the others manoeuvred the prams hurriedly in figure eights around each other like bumping cars at the carnival, and headed in the direction of the Irish House. "You're a bit young yet to be following in your father's footsteps."

The Irish House had round towers and Irish wolfhounds and harps and Erin go Bragh all over it and the name J. O'Meara above the door. I looked down as we passed the entrance but couldn't see my dad's footsteps. Around to the quays and under the three brass balls of O'Gorman's pawnshop we went before crossing the road to the riverside where, way down, over the grey stone wall, ran the River Liffey. I couldn't see over the wall – it was too high for me – but I could smell the low tide of it. Sea gulls whirled and squealed and dived, arguing about who would get what from the mud below.

The nameplates on the walls of the buildings marked our journey: Wood Quay, Essex Quay, Wellington Quay. My mam started to hum a little song to herself, and the rays of the sun painted the iron railings of the Ha'penny Bridge gold. I was happy. "Mam," I said, "when I grow big, I'm going to marry you, do you know that?" Stopping, she looked down at me for a minute, then took her hankie from her sleeve and wiped my nose for me. With a laugh, she tossed her head like she was a horse leading a parade and off she went again. We turned at O'Connell Bridge and went into the swanky interior of Bewley's Coffee House, where the cakes waited for you on their double-decker plates. Pay as you eat. I had never seen such grandeur. Dark wood, marble tables, glass partitions, hanging lamps; the air thick with the coaxing smells of coffee being ground, roasted, percolated and poured. And in spite of all that coffee smell, my mam had a pot of tea. "Have a cake," she said to me. "Or a Club Milk. You can have a fizzy lemonade, too, if you want." She took off her hat and shook out her brown hair. "I'll bet poor old St Blaise never knew what hit him. He's probably asking to be moved to another department this very minute." She winked an eye as she reached for the cake plate. I was awestruck at the idea that even the saints in heaven weren't safe from the jinx that was Jacko.

20

ND THEN I turned four years of age and was sent to Gavan
Duffy's School. Gavan Duffy's wasn't even a boys' school;
it was a girls' school that boys could go to only until they
were seven and then they'd be turfed out. I couldn't wait to be
seven.

We climbed the lavender-polish-smelling stairs that first day, my
mam and me, my damp hand clasped in her cool one, to a big
room overflowing with other boys and girls and desks. A fat lady
wrote my name in a big book, then slammed it shut with a clap as
though she had me trapped in that book for ever. She said she was
sure we'd get along famously, so we would. Whatever gave her that
idea? Could I speak Irish, she wanted to know. As it happened, I
could, a little. I told her the first words I ever uttered were Irish
words, but I spoke so quietly she had to get me to repeat myself.
She seemed pleased and asked what the words were. Pointing up
at the ceiling, I said, *"Féach, réaltaí sa spéir."*

She looked very impressed, and I felt good, happy to have made
her happy. When she asked me to translate it for the others,
though, the smile left my face. I couldn't remember what the
words meant. Maybe I never knew. Maybe I was just repeating
something my dad or someone had said and they weren't my
words at all.

"It means, look, stars in the sky, doesn't it?" she prompted. Yes,
I nodded. Yes, of course, that's what it means, yes. But in truth, if
she had said it meant that Jacko was a bockety bollix, I'd have said
yes to that, too. She told me I was a good boy and to sit at that desk
over there and we'd have a nice day together, all of us. That idea
didn't appeal to me at all. I'd rather go home, so I would. But
when I looked around for my mam, she wasn't there. Smiling, the
teacher pointed out my place again, behind a long desk at the end
of a bench on which several other dazed-looking little ones were

already parked. Tentatively I sat down, but when the teacher looked away, I sneaked over to the window. My mam was threading her way across the playground through a milling crowd of boys and girls. She was going home! Without me!

I made a burst for the door, but the teacher must have been expecting that. For all her bulk, she was fast on her feet. Before I even got my hand on the doorknob, she had headed me off. Kicking and screaming, I was dragged back to the desk and told to stay there. I was a big boy now, she said; if I behaved, my mother might come back for me. I didn't like the sound of that, *might.* I blubbered until my mam did come for me and sulked for the rest of the evening at home. It was the worst day of my whole life, and I could hardly believe it when I was told I had to go again the next day. And the next day after that. What? Did she mean for the whole year? Aye! And the year after that. "Stop being such a baby," she said. "You're a big boy now." Everybody was telling me I was a big boy now, except that at the school I discovered differently. At school, I was neither a big boy nor a little boy; I was a mixed infant. And it wasn't even the real school I was to be in. The next day, along with the rest of the mixed infants, I was herded into a class in a small building at the other end of the playground. The class was called Low Babies; so I was a low baby mixed infant. Next year, I'd be a high baby mixed infant. It didn't seem to be much of a goal.

But – especially as there wasn't anything I could do about it anyway – I sort of accepted the situation. Reluctantly. But not without my own form of protest. For one thing, I made my mam work much harder in the mornings. Where I used to get up early to watch the day get started, now I lay in bed until called. And it wasn't easy to get me to wake up: I could keep my eyes screwed tight shut through a good many shakes before allowing myself to be dragged reluctantly into the light of day. Maybe I had to go to school, but it was somebody else's job to get me there. And if it seemed that my mam might be going to sleep in, I'd be delighted. 'Cause, if she didn't call me in time, it'd be too late for me to go to school. She rarely did sleep in, though, so I couldn't depend on that. Instead, I developed a range of morning sicknesses that would last until a miraculous recovery at around ten o'clock allowed me to go out and play on the banks of the canal for the rest of the day. "I'm going to take you to the Eye and Ear Hospital to find if it isn't just sick of school you are," my mam said.

Obviously I was going to have to work harder at this sickness stuff, and so, whatever about my application at school, I became a very good student at the hospital examinations. If I was a bit vague on the way in as to what was wrong with me, by the time the doctor had asked a few questions – "Does your tongue feel like leather in the morning?" "Is it sore if I press here?" – I had a set of symptoms all ready for tomorrow's performance.

"Oh, Mam, me tongue feels like a lump of leather. Like they said at the I'near Hospital." It didn't always work, though. Once, in spite of having run through all the symptoms I'd picked up at my hospital studies, I was going to be sent to school anyway – so I held on to the banisters and wouldn't let go. They tugged and threatened and bullied and pulled until the pyjama jacket was ripped off me. Half the street came in to offer advice, and I knew I was making a show of myself, but it had gone too far now for me to care. I stuck to that post like a limpet.

Jacko's mam said, "Jayzis, missus. You should leave him there, so you should. Have him shellacked and use him as a hat rack."

Mr O'Connor said, "Put him on exhibition, like in the museum. Charge money in to see him. And do y'know what you could call him? I have the very name. Nude Defending a Staircase." He laughed that hard at his stupid joke he could hardly get another word out, and I hoped he'd choke. But I wouldn't budge, not even when Bermo's dad came and flicked his belt at me like a lion tamer.

"B'gor now," he said when he saw the belt was having no effect. "Do you know what it is, but I have a hacksaw next door. If we was to cut the arms and legs offa him, we could lug him to school in a sack." I reasoned that as I wouldn't be able to write in my copy book without arms, Bermo's dad was probably bluffing. Mind you, from the look on my own dad's face, I wasn't sure but that he might be willing to go along with the idea.

Bermo's mam said, "Like I said, the first-born, a bit . . ." and she

did a sort of fluttery thing with her hand and mouthed the word,
". . . bockety."

I'd show them bockety, so I would. And I did. That day I won.
The grown-ups drifted off about their business, one by one, until
only my mam was left. When she finally said, "Oh, I give up," and
left, I felt safe. But I hung on to the banisters for a bit longer just
in case.

21

HOWEVER, AS I was going to have to go to school anyway, I came to the conclusion that kicking and screaming about going was a waste of time. Apart from anything else, I didn't have the stamina for it that I'd had when I was younger. And when I actually considered it, I had to admit that school wasn't really all that bad. For one thing, I'd made some new friends. Morris and Woolie were two boys who were great gas. In the mornings, my mam and me would go along the canal and meet up with them and their mams at Charlemont Street Bridge. From there, Morris, Woolie and myself would run along the canal bank while the mams followed behind to make sure we didn't have too good a time. But after a couple of weeks, they figured it was safe enough and left us to make our own way to school, and that was much better.

We'd turn off from the canal on to Harcourt Terrace. There was a police station there, and the guards would sometimes stand to attention and salute as we went by. Who would have thought that boys who went to school were that important? They all seemed to have big, round, red faces, the guards did, and talked with the funny accents of their home towns down the country. Sometimes they'd let us boys jump on and off the running boards of their patrol cars, playing cops and robbers. One day, one of them decided that I was a robber, said I was under arrest, and tried to stuff me into the back of the car. The training I'd had at the banisters stood me in good stead that day, because the guard couldn't get me into the car. I held on to the door frame with mighty little fists and screamed so loudly that more guards came running out of the station to see who was being murdered. Two imposing-looking men who had just come out of a house across the road stopped to watch.

"What are you doing to that child, at all at all?" said one of the men in a deep, rumbly voice that filled the street.

"Oh, good day, sir," said the guard, setting me on the ground again. "Just having a bit of fun with the boy."

"Are you indeed?" the man rumbled, sounding amused. "Well now, I'm all in favour of having a bit of fun with the boys myself, so I am."

"Now, Michael, please!" said the other man sternly, like he was warning the first man about something. This man had a big nose and a posh, Englishy sort of voice.

"Oh, now, sir," the guard said, sounding a little embarrassed. "Not that kind of . . . Aren't you the terrible man altogether?"

As the two men walked along Harcourt Terrace toward the canal, the rumbly-voiced one was saying, "That's the trouble with you, Hilton. You might have a sense of humour, but you have no sense of fun." I stared, eyes and mouth wide open, all thoughts of arrest forgotten. Even from across the road, I could see that the man with the rumbly voice was wearing make-up on his face like a woman.

22

THE SUGGESTION CAME from Morris, egged on by Woolie. Why didn't I throw Assumpta Jordan's gloves over the playground wall? It sounded like a good idea to me. Teach her a lesson. Keep her from following us around; getting in the way; wanting to join in our games. If I hesitated for a moment, it was only because I wondered why I was being given the honour. "Course, maybe you're scared," said Morris. That did it. Me, scared of a girl?

Her face brightened as I crossed the schoolyard, and it was no problem to grab the gloves which were tucked inside out into one another. A quick underarm toss and they went sailing over the wall that was maybe three times the height of myself. I turned to see what Morris and Woolie thought of the throw – they weren't there. They'd beaten it. I knew from the frowny look of her that the girl was going to scream any second, so I thought I'd better beat it myself – fast. The roar came when I was only halfway along the playground. Boys-o-boys, but she had lungs.

Next thing I was up before the headmistress; teaching the big girls on the top floor she was, so I had an audience, making the shame ten times worse. Head bowed in front of the class, I stood, hands behind my back, while she read the riot act. In Irish! Not understanding what she was saying, how was I supposed to answer? Whenever she left a meaningful pause – which I didn't know the meaning of – I grunted and nodded solemnly. At last, she stopped talking. There was a long silence which obviously was mine to break. I couldn't just keep looking at the ground, saying nothing, so I couldn't. Slowly I raised my head, cleared my throat, pointed at the ceiling and came out with the only bit of Irish that came to mind: "*Féach, réaltaí sa spéir.*"

"Girls! Girls! Stop laughing." The headmistress was shouting at the class. "He's more to be pitied than laughed at, so he is." She turned her attention back to me. "Are you being cheeky or is it that you haven't understood what I've been saying?" She sighed. "Well, I'm not going to go through it all again, so I'm not. Just let me say that you're a little bully, and if you don't go and get the child's gloves, you'll have to buy her a new pair. Do you understand that?"

I thought I did. "You want me to climb over the wall after them, is that it?" More laughter from the big girls.

"No, it certainly is not it," said the headmistress above the row. "We're not going to have you climbing over walls into people's private property like a thief in the night." There didn't seem to be anything to be gained by pointing out that it wasn't night, so I held my tongue. "You will pretend you're civilised, and you will knock on the door, so you will. You will tell them the naughty thing you have done and hope they're nice people. Fiona, go along with him." She waved a dismissive hand, and Fiona, one of the big girls from the class, held the door for me before closing it on the giggles and the grins. Then she covered her mouth with her hands like she was going to burst and ran to the end of the hall where she let the laugh out.

"Well, you little monkey," she said gleefully and skipped, laughing, all the way down the stairs to the front door. I didn't feel so bad now; making people laugh was all right. At least they weren't angry when they laughed. But at the front door the worry came back again when Fiona pointed the way but didn't move off the step herself. It seemed I was on my own.

Taking a deep breath, I went down the five steps to the footpath. It dawned on me that this was the first time I'd been at the front of the school. Everyone – at least everyone I knew – entered by the back entrance down Hatch Lane. As I looked up at the school, I realised in amazement it wasn't even a real school. It was just a house in a row of other houses – a big, old house converted into a school. Eyes on the ground so as not to step on a crack – step on a crack and break your mother's back – I reached the bottom step to the house next door. It crossed my mind that I should make a run for it, but the big girl was probably expecting that and would catch me, just like the teacher on the first day. Anyway, I didn't know where I was. If I wanted to find my way home, I'd have to go through the school and out the back door. Not a good plan of escape at all. Up I went with heavy steps and pushed on the bell. As a faint ringing sounded from deep inside, a nightmare vision grabbed hold of me. What if this building, too, had been converted into a school and was all classrooms with battered desks, and chalk dust floating in shafts of weak sunlight, and half-cleaned blackboards, and the place full of cane-swishing old teachers all waiting eagerly just for me? I almost did run then, but the opening of the door froze me on the spot. In the doorway was a girl in a maid's uniform, who didn't seem to be much older than Fiona on the step next door. Glancing over in that direction, I caught a glimpse of her bobbing back out of sight into the school doorway. Taking a deep breath, I explained what I had come for, but either she was deaf or my voice had gone quiet again, for she had to get down on her hunkers to hear. She stood and said I'd better come in, so I had. The door swung closed behind me, and I was left alone in the dim hall. It took a moment for my eyes to get used to it, but when they did . . . Boys-o-boys! I was in another world.

There were crossed spears on the walls. And lion skins. And zebra hides. And tiger pelts. Over an arch halfway along the hall was the head of something with twisted horns. A fox, unmoving, watched me from a glass case on the hall table. From its own case opposite, a brown bird with a long tail kept a wary eye on the fox. And halfway up the wall, a speckled fish was frozen in a leap, looking puzzled, like he wondered where the river had gone to.

A door creaked and a man's voice, sounding gruff but posh at the same time, said, "What is it, Mary?" Mary reappeared, gestured toward me and stood back. The man stepped forward into the arch where I could see him and stood under the head with the twisted horns. "Well?" he said. He had a mass of grey hair and carried a pipe. His silvery jacket had a dark collar and was tied at his waist by a tasselled cord. In sharp contrast to the grey hair, his bushy eyebrows were jet black tufts on a sun-browned face. Definny a big game hunter. Words started pouring from me, but the man made an impatient arc in the air with his hand, the smouldering pipe leaving a trail of sweet-smelling smoke behind it. "Don't mumble, man," he said. "Speak up."

I spoke up and sped up, tripping over my tongue as I went. "Gloves . . . Girl's . . . Wall . . . Fell over."

"What? A girl fell over the wall?"

"No." I cleared my throat. "Her gloves."

"She fell over her gloves? You're not making sense, man." From somewhere within my trembling self, I found a voice that was only a little squeaky. "Her gloves fell over the wall." The man puffed quietly on the curved pipe, then he rubbed the bowl of it along the side of his nose. "Very tall girl, is she," he said eventually, examining the pipe bowl where he'd nuzzled it against his face, "that she was able to drop her gloves over a seven-foot wall, eh?" Only he didn't say girl; he said gal.

After a long pause, while the man puffed away, sending up little smoke signals like an Indian Brave calling for help, I said, "I . . . I . . . I threw the gloves over the wall, and I have to get them back."

"You did what?" The man hadn't raised his voice, but somehow the tone made it sound loud. "Why the devil did you do that?" Luckily I didn't have to try and explain because the man went on. "Dare say she deserved it, what? Hah! Now I expect you have to marry her, eh?" For some reason, this terrified me more than anything else that had happened since the whole rotten episode began. With a laugh, the man said, "Maybe I should offer you a tot of whiskey. Steady your nerves, what? Mary will show you the way to the garden. Good hunting."

He turned on his heels and went back, chuckling, to wherever it was he had come from on the other side of the antler-headed arch. I followed the girl through the house that had plants all over it – there were even trees in big pots – until she opened the door leading to the garden.

And what a garden. All overgrown with hanging trees that trailed to the ground half hiding stone benches and statues in their private shade. There were bushes and shrubs and flowers and pathways like a park. Near the door, right out in the open, like it was such a special place that it didn't even rain here like in the rest of Dublin, were a table and chairs. With trees inside and tables and chairs outside, it was like the house was inside out. Birds flashed through the trees, and there was a pond with fishes in it that were even more goldy than the roaches in the canal. For a long moment, I stood mesmerised, forgetting the reason for being here, until a polite cough came from the girl in the uniform. She was pointing down the garden. Along the path, the grey woollen gloves were lying as innocent as you please beside the wall, in a clump of small yellow flowers.

Returning the gloves to Assumpta Jordan, I apologised as I'd been told to, but with my fingers crossed behind my back so the apology wouldn't count. That should teach her a lesson not to keep following us. But it didn't. In fact, now it was even worse. Somehow hadn't one of the yellow flowers got mixed up with the gloves. A soppy smile brightened her face when she saw it. In panic, I fled to the boys' toilet, the laughing voice of the man next door ringing in my head. "Now I expect you have to marry her, eh?"

23

A COUPLE OF times a week, the milk cart came along Portobello Road. Set on two wheels, the cart was nearly all milk
churn with a space behind for the milkman in his crisp
white apron to stand holding the reins of the glossy pony that was
between the shafts in front in a gleaming leather harness. At each
house where a boy or girl or a person ran out with a milk can, the
pony, knowing the ropes, halted. And when you got close and got
a good look at the wagon, you could appreciate how spick the
whole thing was kept. The two iron-rimmed wooden wheels, each
taller than I was, were painted red with a fine green line around
the edge and down along the spokes. The milk churn itself was a
darkly varnished wooden barrel with a shining steel band around
the middle like a belt about a fat man. The rivets were brass and
the handles were copper and the tap shone like gold. Polished
measuring cups hung from its side by their long handles: quarter-
pints, half-pints – pints even, for those who could afford it. Lifting
the lid, the milkman would dunk the dipper into the milk and
ladle it into your can. If the mood was on him, he'd give you a wink
and an extra splash. A tilly, he called it.

Once a week, the slop man came by in his cart, collecting feed
for the pigs he kept somewhere on the other side of the canal. And
not too far away either, because in warm weather, if the wind was
from the right quarter, the aroma of pigsty came wafting over the
water at you. You didn't need the wind when the slop man came
to visit; he carried that same smell right to your door on his
clothes. My nose twitched when he got close, but the smell obviously didn't bother him. He was a happy-looking fellow with a
round face and thick glasses and two big ears that stuck out at right
angles to his head so that from the back he reminded you of a
soup tureen with big handles. The gap-toothed mouth was a sight,
with large, tobacco-stained front teeth. He looked sort of like a

half-blind, jolly rabbit. But not from the neck down; from the neck down, he looked like a tattered rag doll. Coat and trousers were torn and filthy with slimy marks and stains from who knew what. And he stank. "Macgillycuddy Reeks and the slop man stinks," said my mam. But he could do a trick with his nose that I greatly envied. Seated up there on his creaky cart, coat-tails trailing in the ooze behind him, with a little finger placed against one nostril, he could make a green gollier fly out the other, bull's-eye, into the gutter. The one time I tried it, I got snots all up my sleeve.

If the milk cart was a sparkling pride and joy, this cart was the exact opposite. Manky dirty this one was, with wheels so bockety they looked like they'd fall off before the end of the road as the cart creaked and wobbled along. Nor was it pulled by a smart pony in gleaming harness but by a bedraggled donkey in a frayed rope halter who was made to giddy-up with a stick. If you ever wanted to follow that cart, it would be dead easy, because a dribbling trail of ooze marked its path along the road. Actually, even if you were blindfolded, you could follow it, for long after the cart had departed in a cloud of flies, the aroma remained.

"Have you got me bucket for me?" the slop man would ask, the happy grin revealing the ruined ramparts of his teeth. You'd nod without breathing, keeping your lips closed. My mam – as did most of the mams on the street – kept a bucket of slops under the sink for the slop man. Into this bucket went the scrapings off the plates as well as the bits and scraps that weren't fit for the stew: potato peelings, manky tomatoes, ends of carrots, onion skins, tea leaves, eggshells, congealed rasher fat, blue bread, fuzzy apples, grizzle – the lot. Not to mention the odd cigarette butt off the side of my dad's plate. And all of it the slop man would take home with him to feed his pigs. Sometimes when you were handing it over, there'd be a rustle from the bucket, and you knew one of your mice was about to change his residence.

Whistling, the slop man would waddle to his cart and toss in the contents of the bucket. Splosh! More splatters would fly upward to land on his clothes and speckle his glasses. If they got rightly covered, he'd take the glasses off and, with his eyes scrunched up to the size of pin heads, smear the lenses around in the end of his moth-eaten jumper, held between finger and thumb. Before he came back with your empty bucket, in case he wanted to talk, you took a deep breath as protection against the smell of him. Then you carried on a conversation without breathing. You nodded a lot and said uhuh a lot, so as not to waste air, but if the slop man was feeling chatty – finally, as you turned blue – you'd have to spin away and take another deep breath of fresh air from your hallway before turning back again with your cheeks bulging. You hoped that now you had enough air to see you through, because after a couple of spins and swallows, you started to feel light-headed and dizzy, and you'd think of the stories you'd heard about deep-sea divers and how they sometimes got the bends from bad air or something and died roaring.

It was the donkey I felt sorry for. Did he have a stall of his own, I wondered, or did he have to sleep with the pigs? Did he ever get to smell a flower; or anything at all other than pigs and pig-slop the whole time? Did he ever get a cube of sugar or a pat from the children he visited? Or was he so dirty and smelly that they always stayed back and wouldn't go near him? Did that poor donkey, a quietly suffering saint, spend his whole life pulling a bockety cart through the streets of Dublin, his head encircled in a halo of flies? He who takes away the skins of the world.

24

UNCLE BILL SOMETIMES called at our house on his way home from work. Recognising his bald head in the distance, I would run to meet him so I could cycle half his bicycle along Portobello Road. You cycled half a bicycle by standing on one pedal while your uncle worked the other one, sending you up and down as the bike went forward. "If I ever lose a leg," my uncle said, "I'm going to hire you to help me ride the bike."

I thought this might be possible. He'd already lost his hair; who knew what might be next? I had been intrigued by his big, shiny scalp ever since I could remember. "I was born with a full head o' hair," he told me, "but by the time I was twenty-six, I was bald as a coot."

My uncle often had advice about whatever game I might be playing. "If you were to move those Indians around behind yon shoe box, you could capture those cowboys there."

"It's not a shoe box; it's a fort; and the Indians are the baddies, not the cowboys."

"Och, now, maybe the Indians aren't as bad as they're painted. Some of those cowboys were no prizes, I can tell you." Uncle Bill had an accent that was like my mam's, on account, my dad said, of them both being from the black North. My dad said Uncle Bill was my mam's half brother. This was obviously a joke; Uncle Bill was fat enough to be a brother and a half. He worked in Wills' cigarette factory on the South Circular Road, which wasn't too far away from our house, so it was no bother to him to drop in sometimes – and always with a packet of free cigarettes for my mam. These came disguised in a white packet because they were test cigarettes that they tried out on their workers first to make sure they were safe enough to sell.

"They give us free cigarettes to keep us hooked for fear we'd give up smokin' on them," said my uncle, as he puffed away contentedly along with my mam. "What sort of advertising would it be if the workers wouldn't smoke their fags?"

"A good job he has, too, your uncle," my mam told me. "An electrician is a good job. You could do worse than follow your Uncle Bill's example." There seemed to be a bit of bad feeling between my dad and my uncle. Something about money owing and having to close down the shoe shop in Inchicore. But it didn't stop him from visiting, nor did it stop us going over on St Stephen's Day to the house in Donnycarney where Uncle Bill lived with Granma and Granda. St Stephen's Day was the day they gave out the Christmas presents, and after I ceased to be an only, I often felt I got the wrong present. Once I got a football and my brother got the gun and holster I'd wanted. Another time, the fire engine I had my eye on didn't come my way either. There were often tears on Stephen's Day.

"Och! Stop girnin'. You're actin' like a wee babby," my mam would say then, her Northern accent more noticeable when she was angry. I liked the accent with the "Ochs" and "Ayes" and loved when we went to the North where everybody spoke that way. It was like going on holiday to a foreign country. Not that I felt like a foreigner. I had relatives all over and, best of all, on Rathlin Island. Rathlin Island was deadly. All high, windy cliffs and sky, it was just about as far away from Dublin as you could get – the next stop was Scotland. My mam had lived there when she was a wee girl, and when we went there, she seemed not so much like a mam any more; she was brighter or something. And more lively. If there was a *céilí* in the hall down at the harbour, she danced all night and never got tired. And she laughed a lot. Even when I sat on an ant hill, she laughed. I didn't think it was a bit funny, across her knees out there in the open by the side of the dirt road with my pants down while she hunted for ants on me. I roared at her angrily to stop laughing, but she said she wasn't laughing at me at all but at the ants. Comical ants she said they were, up to all kinds of *antics*. She laughed even louder.

25

VAST, GREY AND grimy-domed, Amiens Street Station was alive with scurrying people and big swaying carriages behind powerful, clanking engines straining to be off to somewhere else. The place smelt of smoke and the engines hissed steam and dripped water and ticked and spat as hot metal cooled. We were going to Rathlin Island, my dad and me.

He lifted me up from the platform into the carriage, swung the suitcase into an overhead rack made of holes joined together like a fishing net, worked the strap that lowered the window, and I had a good view of the goings-on on the platform. Pigeons swooped down from crossed girders high above and landed in front of a man pushing a brushful of dust from one end of the platform to the other. Like they were searching for their carriage, the pigeons strutted along the length of the train for a bit before leaping into the air again to hitch a lift on an iron-wheeled luggage cart being pulled by two men in peaked caps. Beside big gates, a wooden crate was being hoisted off a horse-and-cart and on to a luggage cart. The crate gave me a creepy feeling; it was just the size and shape to hold a body. Even creepier, the horse wore a straw hat and looked at me in an odd way, as though he knew something about this trip I didn't.

With the screech of a whistle and a hiss of steam, the train jerked forward so that the man about to light up in the seat opposite missed his pipe and nearly poked the match into his eye. The train stopped as though it had only sneezed. It sneezed forward again. And again. And we really were on our way this time. Out from the dusty dimness of the station, the engine sent its plume of smoke up into a grey, rainy sky streaked and smudged like wet blotting paper. My dad made a dive and pulled up the window to keep the rain out.

Past the grimy backyards of the city centre the train steamed.

Over the muddy water of the Tolka it chugged, and by the bleak empty field of Fairview Park. Clontarf's long back gardens were next, where Brian Ború got his head chopped off by the Danes. "Down on his knees muttering prayers," said my granda, "instead of looking after business." Killester now, gardens adrip with limp washing on sagging clothes lines. Over bridged sea-fingers and by Portmarnock, Malahide, Skerries, Balbriggan, the telephone wires dipping and rising between the poles, the clack of the wheels changing tone and missing a beat with each pole they passed. The train was going so fast now, the raindrops dashed across the window-pane at a steep angle.

At one station we came to, a woman getting out of the carriage was in such a hurry she slammed the door on my fingers. The roar out of me got everyone's attention, except the woman's. She was running off down the platform, coat and handbag flying, hand to her head, holding her feathered hat in place. Someone in the carriage gave me a bag of sweets, which made me forget about the pain and stopped my crying. When I glanced up from examining the bag's contents, I noticed that everyone was looking at me sympathetically. In embarrassment, before I could stop myself, I went around the carriage, offering everyone a sweet. I hadn't meant to do that. The last thing I wanted was to give away the sweets I'd nearly lost my fingers over, but nobody took one, so that was all right. And now everyone thought I was very nice, and that was even better.

"Here they come, bad cess to them," somebody said as we puffed into a station near the border. It was the customs men he was talking about. They climbed on to the train and moved along its length, tension going before them like the wave in front of a canal barge. The stern-faced officials came through our carriage asking a question here, opening a suitcase there. "*Achtung*," someone said, causing a bit of a titter; but the man who said it got his suitcase thoroughly examined for his joke. The word sounded interesting. I was getting ready to try it out myself, but my dad must have seen my lips moving into position, for he hissed at me not to bloody-well dare. I offered the customs man a sweet and was surprised when he took one.

"Och, thanks, wee lad." He poked two gloved fingers, scissor-like, deep into the bag. As he sucked, he made a chalk mark on our case without opening it and moved to the next car. The man who had said *Achtung* wanted to know if I was for rent and made everybody laugh. Now it was like a party, with everyone telling stories about what they had got away with in the past.

One man told of a fellow – "Not me you understand? A man I knew, you understand?" – who had a special coat with a plastic lining that could hold pounds and pounds of butter. "He was gettin' away with bringin' butter across the border for months, so he was. But wan day, a real hot day it was too, you understand? Wasn't there some sort of a hold-up and he had t'sit for ages. What with the special coat on him, wasn't he sweatin' buckets? And, o' course, with the heat of the day and the heat comin' offa the man hisself, wasn't the butter gettin' runny, you understand? O' course, it was all too much for the plastic linin'. Drip! Drip! Drip! The man could feel it oozin' out of him into the seat, but he couldn't move because two customs men were standin' near by, smokin' a fag. They didn't leave until the train started, and by then wasn't yer man so buttery that he slid offa the seat onta the floor with the jerk o'the engine. Down the aisle he skittered, slidderin' out of the grasp of everywan what tried to grab a'hold of him. He didn't stop till he ran out of butter."

Carriage doors slammed as the customs men got off the train. A whistle blew. Looking out the window, I saw a guard at the back wave a flag at the driver. And even though we were entering the black North, it was a green flag.

26

ITH A LONG-DRAWN-OUT puff, as though exhausted from the long haul, the train came to a stop in Belfast. Collars up against the rain, we set off for the bus station and the next leg of the journey. As we walked – my dad putting the suitcase down for a rest every couple of streets – the rain ended and the sun came out. Flicking the rain from my cap, I asked my dad where the orange men were. He jammed the cap back on my head, grabbed the suitcase and walked off, saying to keep quiet, that they were probably all around. I looked about curiously but could see only ordinary people. And flags. You never saw flags in Dublin, but here every house seemed to boast a limp, damp Union Jack, steaming now in the weak sunlight.

"Do you know what Armagh said to Ardagh?" We were on the bus, front seat, driver's side, headed for Ballycastle, and my dad was telling me a riddle. "Armagh said to Ardagh, 'If you weren't so Ballymena with your Ballymoney, we could be living in a Ballycastle instead of in a Ballyholme.' Do you get it? Our ma said to our da? They're all towns, you see? If you weren't so bally mean with your bally money . . ." He was still explaining it when the bus conductor came along. "One all the way," he said.

"What about the wee lad?" asked the conductor.

"Him? Ah, no. He's free, under age."

"Is he, now? He looks a bit big to me."

My dad had an arm around me and was squishing me down into the seat as though trying to make me smaller. "Ah, no," he said. "He's just big for his age, that's all."

"What age would that be?"

"He's about, oh, just coming up to five, I think." I hated to see my dad in difficulty and thought I could help him out here.

"No, Dad. I'm seven," I piped up. I was very surprised when everyone started laughing.

"Well, he's a half fare so," said the conductor who, along with my dad, seemed to be the only other person on the bus who didn't think seven a funny age. Peeling two tickets off a little bundle of them, he fed them into a machine at his belt that dinged as it took a bite out of each.

"Sure you're not twenty-seven?" asked my dad. "I don't know these things," he said as he paid the conductor. "His mother's the one keeps track of the birthdays." He was a bit grumpy for a while after that and wasn't telling any more riddles, which was fine by me because it gave me time to examine the surroundings. On the other side of the sliding window in front of us, the driver's little room was chock-a-block with levers and dials and a huge steering wheel wider than the man himself. A cigarette in his mouth, he steered with one hand while the other stuck out the side window and rested on the huge silver headlamp that showed a hall-of-mirrors image of himself. The reflected hand resting on the shiny surface was huge, and the long arm that stretched away from it narrowed down to a tiny, smoking head. Nor was the driver the only one smoking; the air in the bus was full of smoke from the people behind who were puffing away also. A faint smell of petrol mingled with the smoke, all of it cooking slowly in the sun-warmed, swaying oven of a bus. One minute I was looking out the window, and the next, to my great surprise, I was out of the seat like a flash and violently sick down the steps to the door.

"Look at the poor child," a woman said. "For God's sake, will youse open a couple a' windas? It's like a fish-curin' factory in here." Windows slid open as the bus pulled over to the side of the road and stopped. The conductor said I'd shown great presence of mind to puke down the steps, because wasn't he able to get rid of most of it by pushing it out the door with a scrunched-up newspaper. As the bus moved off again he said, "The widow's is on'y a couple o'miles on. We can clean it up a bit better there." With the windows open to air out the bus, I felt a bit better, and a short time later, the driver pulled up at a shop with signs for porter and whiskey on it and wellington boots and rain macs hanging outside. The conductor said we had ten minutes to use the facilities while he got a mop for the steps. The driver clambered down from his cab, and he, the conductor, and nearly everyone else, went into the building. My dad said that in spite of my being seven, he thought he had enough left for a pint, and would I like a bottle of lemonade? He brought it out for me, and when I went in later looking for the lav, I saw that everyone seemed very relaxed and didn't look like they'd be moving for a while.

"Right," the bus conductor was saying from his seat at the bar. "Soon as I finish this one, we're on our way. Cheerio." He held his glass up like the priest at mass and, from force of habit, I blessed myself.

"A wee papist, are ya?" a man in a black hat said. "Aye, I thought that, right enough." My dad sort of flicked at me with the back of his hand like I was a bad smell, and I went back to the bus to wait with the few others that didn't have to use the facilities.

On our way again, my dad was in a singing mood. I tried to make him stop, but he wasn't having any of it. Turning around, he knelt on his seat with his arms crossed on the back of it and spoke to the bus in general. "My son here, my seven-year-old son, says that I'm out of turn. So I'm asking if anyone else wants to sing first? No? There you are, son, you see?" Now I was really embarrassed and sorry that I'd opened my mouth at all. My dad cleared his throat and sang a song about the star of the County Down. Then he sang another one, one about a bailiff and a devil. By this time, I was scrunched so far down in the seat, I'd have had no trouble passing for a five-year-old; only for the bus was moving, I'd have stepped off it in shame. After a few more songs, though, my dad had a bit of a snooze, and slowly the shame ebbed away. Sitting beside the window, open in case – as the bus man said – I got a touch of the collywobbles again, I put a hand out and let the wind whistle through spread fingers. Whenever the bus came to a sign-post for Ballycastle, I checked to make sure the driver was going the right way, because signs were pointing to other Bally places, too. Ballymena. Ballymoney. Ballycastle. Cushendall. The names seemed to fit with the whirr of the wheels. Ballymena. Ballymoney. Ballycastle. Cushendall. Ballymena-Ballymoney-Ballycastle-Cushendall. Ballymena-Ballymoney-Bally . . .

I woke, I don't know how much later, with my dad's arm warm

around me. I sat still, listening to the quiet sounds in the bus: the soft snores of somebody behind me, my dad's breathing, the whirr of the tyres, the creaky sway of the vehicle. I felt secure sitting there close to my dad, smelling the faint, smoky odour of his jacket. Without moving, I asked him, "Why is it that me mam sometimes seems so snarky with you?"

"So you're awake, are you?" He took a deep breath and looked out the window at County Antrim flashing by while his free hand rambled in and out among his pockets until it found his packet of Sweet Afton for him. Another fumbling search found the box of matches. A match flared and the flame was sucked toward the end of the cigarette. Using the thumb and little finger of his left hand – the cigarette clamped between the first two fingers – he removed a piece of tobacco from the tip of his tongue and drew me around in front of him.

"Well, the truth is," he began at last, as he hoisted me on to his knee, "it seems that I'm a bit of a disappointment to your mam sometimes. Not that she doesn't have a point, I agree. I don't seem to have the luck for finding a decent job, for one thing. Oh, I sometimes get some grand schemes all right, but they never seem to work out exactly. But sometimes I wish your mam would be more . . ." He pounded gently on the seat with the side of his closed fist as he searched for the word he wanted. Then, "Aye," he said quietly to himself in apparent agreement with the word he'd found.

"More what, Dad?" I wanted to know.

"Oh, never you mind." He took the cigarette from his mouth and blew a cloud of smoke into the air. "It's not as good as it could be, but probably better than I deserve. She's a good woman, so she is. And a grand mam to you. See that you're not a disappointment to her, and maybe that'll make up for me. Will you promise me that?" I promised, just because it seemed important to my dad. But sure, how could either of us be a disappointment to my mam? Didn't she love us both? In silence, he held me on his knee for the rest of the trip through the green hills to the rocky coast of Antrim.

That night, we stayed just outside Ballycastle in a house on a hill. Lifting the curtains on the upstairs window, I could see what we'd come for: Rathlin Island floating out there on the water. Six miles away, they said, but it looked close enough to swim to. Not that we'd have to swim. Tomorrow we'd take a boat. In bed between crisp sheets up under the sloped roof, I heard the muffled discussion from downstairs, and when they started talking about Bee Specials, it caught my attention. I wondered if they were any relation to the Honey Bees sweets you could get in Dublin? I knew they had different sweets here in the North. Spangles, for one: you couldn't get Spangles in Dublin, and Spangles were deadly. But from the snippets of talk I caught as I drifted off to sleep, I gathered that Bee Specials weren't sweets at all but some class of dangerous animal that was to be found nowhere else in the world but in Northern Ireland.

27

"AYE, WELL! CHECK with Jim Creel." The man behind the bar the next day had been asked about a boat to the island. "He might be going over if the weather eases. Then again, he might not. You never know with Jim. Try the boat-house at the end of the pier."

The day was grey, blustery and squalling with rain. It was late in the morning and me, my dad and the man from the house we had stayed at last night were in a bar in the harbour. "Can I go and find him?" I asked. I wanted to get out of this gloomy place that smelled of stale beer. Other smells, too, swam toward me every time the door of the lav swung open, giving me a queasy feeling in my stomach.

"I suppose so," my dad said. "We can keep an eye on him from here, can't we?" he asked the other man.

"Och, aye. We can see the boathouse through yon window," the man replied. "And isn't he the right wee lad altogether?"

My dad was saying, "The same again," to the barman as I went out the door. Head down, collar up against the rain, glad to be out in the fresh air, I scurried along the quay and down the pier to the boathouse. The place seemed empty, but when I got used to the dim light, I could see a man sitting on a box, knitting an end to a lobster pot. Concentrating as he was on his knitting, the man didn't seem to notice I had come in. Finally I did a pretend cough.

"Aye?" he said, glancing up.

"I was looking for Jim Creel," I said.

"Oh, aye," said the man, going back to his knitting.

After a silence – when I realised he wasn't going to say any more – I asked, "Do you know Jim Creel?"

"Aye. I do." Another silence except for the sound of string squealing against string as he went on knitting.

"Do you know where he lives?"

"Aye. I do."

Again I waited to see was he going to say more. No, it seemed he wasn't. "Well, will you tell me where he lives, please?" I asked, hoping that when I found him, Jim Creel would be friendlier than this fellow.

"Up to the road. Blue door. Number seventeen," the fellow said.

Back on the road, I knocked on the blue door and asked the lady who opened it was Jim Creel there. She said, "Och, look at you, wee lad. You must be soaked. Did you no try the boathouse?" Back at the boathouse it finally dawned on me.

"Are you Jim Creel?" I asked.

"I am indeed, wee lad." And Jim Creel threw back his head and laughed hard as though he was the funniest man in the world. It turned out that, yes, he was going across to the island that afternoon and, yes, there would be room for two more passengers. I hoped he turned out to be a better sailor than he was a comedian.

As soon as the open boat moved from the shelter of the pier wall, the wind hit it with force. Out among them, the waves were much bigger than they'd seemed from the shore. When the boat climbed up the side of one, it toppled over the top with a smack that covered everyone with a drenching spray. And each rapid rise of the prow left my stomach behind, scrambling to catch up. As it plummeted down again into the trough, the sour taste of old breakfast rose to my mouth, but although it came close, I managed to hold it down. Others weren't so lucky. Several of them were hanging over the side, afraid to leave it, and one man hadn't even made it that far. With his head in his hands, he sat moaning as stuff poured out of his mouth over his shoes and splattered the ends of his trousers.

You could tell the ones who weren't going to make it; their faces turned a dirty white – green almost – before they dived for the side. Green for go. I wondered what colour my own face was. Not the same colour as my knees, I hoped, which were orangey-purple-white; I sat hugging them to keep them warm. At least I was dry in under the little bit of a roof at the front of the boat where they'd put me out of the way of the spray. Someone was explaining that

the boat was on a long tack because of the current, and I hoped this long tack didn't come up through the bottom of the boat and sink us all.

Close to the white cliffs of the island, the boat moved easier and didn't buck so much, and when it came into the harbour, the wind dropped like someone had switched it off. Men in raincoats and wellington boots came running down the pier to meet the boat and catch the ropes thrown up to them. I was lifted on to the wet stone steps and wobbled up them to the pier. The unmoving ground felt strange after the pitching and rolling but, wobbly legs or not, I was happy to be there. Where the pier met the land was a house that was a pub on one side of the hallway and the post office on the other. If it had been a boat, it would have tipped over, because just about everybody went into the pub side. My dad said that as Uncle Sandy wasn't here yet, we'd wait for him in this place, and he asked the barman for a bottle of something. The man said they didn't have any of that Free State beer but said to try a – it sounded like, m'gargle. Good name for a drink, I thought. My dad said he'd try one and, after sniffing it and holding it up to the light, took a sip. He worked his mouth like he was chewing on the beer, then swallowed and smacked his lips. Nodding wisely, he said there was a good cut to it right enough. Would I like a lemonade or something, he asked. I wondered should I be asking for it by the name on the bottle like the men did. To say just "a lemonade" seemed very uninformed. Maybe I should ask for a Cantrell and Cochrane, please. Or wait, maybe I'd try a Taylor-Keith today. I decided that was only making things complicated and just said, "Yes, please." And do you know what? There was a good cut to it right enough.

Uncle Sandy came along on a tractor with a trailer of hay behind it, and after he'd had a m'gargle himself, "Just to keep ye company," my dad and me and our suitcase lay on the hay as Uncle Sandy drove away from the harbour. The uphill, dirt road was all muddy-water-filled holes and had a channel down the middle of it that was still running even though the rain had stopped. The trailer bucked and bounced along it like the boat, only without the soaking spray.

Uncle Sandy lived untidily by himself. The attic, even dustier than the rest of the place, was full of things he said had washed ashore over the years. Flotsam and jetsam, he said it was called. "Y'want some flotsam? We got some. Y'want some jetsam? We can get some. Try that for size, wee lad." The heavy, brass telescope he handed me was nearly as tall as me when it was pulled out of itself. From a German submarine, he said it was, and the hole in the side of it was a bullet hole. "And that might be a blood stain there on the leather, see?" This was massive; I was really impressed. A lot of stuff washed up on these rocky shores during the war, he said. A lot of it seemed to have washed right into his house. There was a brass shell casing big enough for me to get a leg into. There was a big ship's compass that stayed level no matter which way you tilted it. But under the grimy, cobwebby little window at the front of the attic was the prize. A large, bronze diving helmet with portholes all around it sat on the floor, glinting dully in the dim light that struggled in through the murky window. Like a giant who had stuck his head through from below to see what was going on, it watched my every move.

Out in the yard later, Uncle Sandy asked if I'd like some chicken for dinner. When I said yes, he turned, kicked out and sent a pecking chicken flying. Then he grabbed it and wrung its neck. Although it wasn't my boot that did the kicking, it might as well have been, because I had caused that murder. At dinner time, I couldn't bring myself to eat the corpse, and that put Uncle Sandy in a bad mood. He went on about how city people were so strange, and where did they think food came from at all? Out of a box? I said no, out of the butcher's. "And where do you think the butcher gets it from, do you mind tellin' me?" he asked. "An' y' probably think milk comes out of a tap? Someone has to do the hard and dirty work for you city people or you'd starve, so you would."

I supposed that yes, the sheep and pigs and cows hanging in the butcher's shop must have been rambling around the fields once, now that I thought about it. I quickly stopped thinking about it. But I knew where milk came from: it came in a gleaming cart pulled by a glossy pony in a fine leather harness.

28

EXT DAY, THE weather had changed, and in the shelter of the harbour at Church Bay it was warm enough for us to swim. The high, fast-moving clouds rushing in front of the sun made the sea outside the bay change colour from green to blue to mauve to white-flecked gold, repeating itself over and over in ever-changing variations. In the bay, the water was clear and inviting. "It's not nearly as treacherous as yesterday," said my dad.

Uncle Sandy took the pipe from his mouth and spat a long jet into the foam. "You're wrong there," he said. "Yesterda' the sea was bein' honest wi' ya. A day when it's smooth an' invitin' lookin' is when it's really bein' treacherous."

Uncle Sandy was a craggy man with bushy eyebrows who didn't seem to have shaved in a while. I watched in fascination as his chin got a little darker with each passing day. Whereas my dad went through the shaving ritual every day, Uncle Sandy didn't even look at a razor. And the rest of the island men seemed to be growing beards too, like they were all monks or something. Until Sunday morning that is; because then wasn't Uncle Sandy shaved clean as a whistle. And so was every other man we passed on the way to mass on the tractor. Evidently they'd all been up early that morning with the Blue Gillettes. All the bearded monks of yesterday had been replaced with clean-shaven men. It was like Jim Creel had delivered a load of razor blades and the shortage was over. But on Monday, the chin shadow was back again, and each day that went by left more stubble behind it. Not one islandman's chin came anywhere near a razor until the next Sunday morning. Even my dad became contaminated and allowed himself a couple of razor-free days near the end of the week.

Rathlin was like no place I'd ever been. In Dublin, there were people everywhere, and buildings, and bicycles, and cars – both horse-drawn and motor. Here there was nothing but the odd tractor, a few houses, sky, grass and birds such as you'd never see in a city. The side of the cliffs was alive with swarms of squabbling seabirds that blacked out the sun when they took off with a clatter of wings like thunder.

On our way to visit the lighthouse, Uncle Sandy told us Bruce's cave was below at the foot of the cliff. This Bruce was a Scottish man who had a pet spider that talked him into taking Scotland back from the English. Uncle Sandy was pointing out the birds to my dad. "Them's razorbills, and guillemots, kittiwakes and puffins," he said, jabbing a finger at each wheeling bird as he named it, like he was trying to pin it in place. I was more interested in the warrior spider and wondered if he was still down there. Looking over the cliff, I saw some blobs of cotton wool on the rocks far below. But no, it couldn't be cotton wool. Then I realised what it was. Sheep! Sheep that had grazed too close to the edge of the cliff and slipped over. With shock, I straightened up suddenly, and my feet went from under me. As I slithered in the footsteps of the slipped sheep, my dad let a roar out of him.

"Jesus Christ," he shouted, lunging after me and grabbing me by the back of my pullover. Uncle Sandy grasped my dad's free hand, and they both hauled me backward to safety. "Christ Almighty," said my dad, hardly able to speak. I could feel his hand shaking where he gripped my pullover; although I was in no danger now, he wouldn't let go. Both he and Uncle Sandy were white. My dad seemed to be having a hard time breathing. "Don't you ever . . . what possessed you to do that . . . what would I tell your mam if I came home without you?"

"That I was dead as mutton?" I said with a shiver and began to cry. My dad put his jacket around me and didn't let go of my hand until we reached the lighthouse.

The lighthouse was the most fabulous building I'd ever been in. As we climbed, each round room was just a little smaller than the one below it. I went up a ladder to the smallest room at the top and poked my head through the floor. The glare in there was blinding, but it wasn't just the windows all round that made it like that. It was the giant magnifying glasses and prisms between me and the windows that had the light so dazzling. And there, tiny but

mighty at the centre of it all, was the light that was the very source
of the lighthouse's being. I was amazed. It was just a little Tilly
lamp like the one Uncle Sandy used in his house. Maybe it had a
few more mantels, but it was basically the same. You pumped it up,
turned a knob and, with a whoosh, lit it with a match.

"This box of matches," said the lightkeeper, taking the box from
his pocket and rattling it in my ear, "is the most important piece
of apparatus in the place. You can tell a true lighthouse man by
the fact that he always carries a box of matches in his pocket."

Across Uncle Sandy's yard and down some steps ran the burn
where he washed the dishes – when he bothered to wash them at
all. One day he took the plates, still with bits of fish from dinner
on them, down the steps, and called up to me, "Come on down
here, wee lad, till I show ya." He had scraped the plates into the
water by the time I got to the bottom of the steps. "Quiet now," he
said and whistled. We waited. Then . . . Boys-o-boys. I was squirming with excitement while Uncle Sandy held me tight to stop me
jumping up and down and scaring away the two large, twisty eels
that came wriggling up the river and stopped right there.

They had come for a visit, Uncle Sandy whispered. "They're my
pet eels, so they are, that'll come when I whistle. What d'you think
o' that?"

I thought eels certainly left the pinkeens of the canal in the
ha'penny place. After a few moments, the fish eaten, the eels nodded at Uncle Sandy and wriggled away. I whistled but they
wouldn't come back for me. Uncle Sandy said the accent was
wrong. North of Ireland eels just wouldn't answer to a Free State
whistle, he said.

29

PRESSED AGAINST THE squinty window, I saw him belting along the road on his bicycle and had the door open before the knock came. This was unusual. Uncle Bill never called to the house this early in the day. There were no smiles from him and he didn't come in, just called over my head for my mam. "Give that to her," he said to me, pushing a bag at me. "She'll understand. I'm on me way to work." Then he threw himself across his bike and pedalled along the canal in the direction of Bloomfield Avenue.

The bulging bag was heavy and made of rough, blue-grey stuff with straps that buckled on the front, and it was heavy. I put it on the floor and hunkered down to examine it. One of the straps wasn't pulled all the way tight, and I slipped a hand in under the flap and felt . . . a gun? Yes! Something else in there, too. Another gun? But, definny, at least one gun. I knew what a gun felt like because I had a cowboy gun and holster of my own. Only this one felt much bigger. As I was starting to unbuckle the strap to take a look, my mam came along.

"Mam! Mam!" I said, all excited. "That's a gun, so it is. A gun." Was Uncle Bill a cowboy like Roy Rogers?

"Don't be silly," said my mam, taking the bag. "It's just some tools from your uncle's work, is all it is. Here, go and get yourself a square of Cleeve's Toffee." I looked from the bag to the ha'penny in her hand. Maybe Honey Bees, I thought, not Cleeve's Toffee. When I came back from Lynch's, I had one Honey Bee left and there was no sign of the bag.

I noticed my mam was a bit worried looking for the rest of the day, and when my dad came in that evening, he looked at her funny and asked her what was the matter. "Nothing," she said brightly. "What would be the matter?"

"I don't know," he said. "You just look a bit . . . I don't know, distracted."

"Och, I suppose I'm worried about your job. You being out of work next week."

"Well, yes," he said. "But I have an idea. I was thinking about going back into the shoe business, only specialising this time. I made some cycling shoes one time for a racing man when I had the shop, and he was very pleased with them. I used different-coloured soft leathers for the uppers and I put some cleats on the soles to grip the pedals. Gave him the extra speed, d'you see? And I was thinking of maybe going in with someone who was already in the racing-bike trade. What do you think of that?"

"That sounds fine and dandy. If you could make a go of it."

"Give me credit, woman. Of course I can make a go of it. With a bit of luck."

"Of course. I didn't mean . . ."

"If you had a bit of faith in me sometimes, it'd be a help."

"Oh, I do. I do have faith in you. If you could only . . ."

"Only what?"

"Nothing." She stopped talking, like she was a wireless that had just been switched off in the middle of a sentence. His face went stiff. She drew in her breath and changed the subject, sounding bright and friendly. And false. "I have your dinner in the oven. Do you want me to bring it up to you?"

He gave a loud sigh and said, "No, I don't want you to bring it up to me. Somehow the appetite's left me. I'm going out for a bit." He left the room and I heard the front door open and the whirr of bicycle wheels going backward along the hall. There was the noisy scrape of the pedal against the wood of the door. "Dammit to hell," I heard him say and then the door slammed behind him.

". . . If you could only steer clear of the pubs and the ponies," my mam said to nobody in particular, the wireless switched on again.

When the tap came on the window a little later, I was under the table playing with my cowboys and Indians. My mam seemed to have forgotten I was there, so I just sat quietly to see what was going to happen next.

"What's wrong, Bill?" she said at the door.

"Is he in?" my uncle asked.

"Not at all," she answered. "Down in Clarke's for the evening, I'd say."

"I'm nearly bunched," he said.

"Come in and sit down at the fire and have a cup of tea."

I grabbed a cowboy that had wandered too far and pulled him back into the shadows with me in case he gave the game away. Uncle Bill and my mam came into the sitting room and sat on either side of the fire. All I could see of them was their legs in the glow of the flames. There was the rustle of a cigarette packet and the scrape and flash of a match. The deep intake of breath from my uncle as he pulled on his cigarette was followed by the sound of a slow exhale and a stream of smoke spewed downward. Uncle Bill's hand came into view as it tossed the screwed-up silver paper from the cigarette package into the fire. My mam's thumb flicked at the end of her cigarette, sending the ash tumbling to the hearth. They sat in silence until finally my uncle said, "I plugged a man yesterday."

I nearly came out from under the table when he said that – plugged. Just like a cowboy picture at the Prinner. *Yeah, sure I plugged him. He had it comin', the dirty, rotten, no-good horse thief.* But I didn't move; the tension in the room kept me from moving.

"Oh, Bill," my mam said. "Where?"

"Up near Creggan. I got back early this morning." There was another silence before he went on again. "It was supposed to be an interrogation. It wasn't an interrogation. It was just cold-blooded, fucking torture. They had the poor bastard across the table and were putting live coals in his mouth. Imagine. They said they wanted to make him talk and what do they do? They burn his mouth away. The smell of burned flesh; and naturally he'd shit himself so there was that smell too. And the bastards were enjoying it. They really were. Pretending to be fighting for Ireland and really they're just sick monsters. They're not the same now, the people who are coming in nowadays. The honour and glory of Ireland my arse. If the people of Ireland knew . . . It made me ashamed to be fighting for the cause, so it did.

"'Ah, Bill,' says one of them in his high, nasal, Belfast whine. 'You're just in time. Would you care for a light for your fag?' And he held out the tongs with a red-hot coal in it, a big grin on his mug. The poor bastard on the table had his head turned my way, but I knew he couldn't see me. His eyes were just pools of ashy tears. He was trying to speak too, but sure his tongue must have been nearly gone by this. And his lips were just huge, raw blisters. I couldn't stand it. I leaned over, said a quick act of contrition in his ear, and shot him. I had to. Just to put him out of his torment. I had to." In the long silence that followed, I didn't even breathe. At last, my Uncle Bill went on. "The other two boyos were furious. 'You come all the way up from Dublin because you're supposed to be useful, and all you can do is pull a trigger. He wasn't yours. He was ours. We'd have done him when we were through.' He was that furious, the spittle was all over his chin like a mad dog. I came that close to letting him have it too. Pointed the gun between his piggy little eyes and came that close. He went pale and started whinge-ing for mercy. I'm not sure if I did the right thing or not but, God forgive me, I didn't shoot him."

"Oh, Bill," my mam said. "Poor Bill."

"Aye, poor Bill is right," he said, and there was another long silence. "Hide the bag for me," he said at last. "I'll be back for it, but I have some thinking to do first."

When they went to the front door, I saw that the cowboy still clutched in my hand was trembling. I scurried upstairs to bed but had a hard time getting to sleep, and when I finally did, it was to dream of smoky, tongueless men, screaming soundlessly and spew-ing red-hot coals from the black holes of their mouths. I woke ter-rified. In the dream, I'd had to plug someone and couldn't get the right prayer. I couldn't remember which one was the act of con-trition. Was it the "I confess to almighty God" one? Or the "Oh, my God I am heartily sorry for having offended thee" one? Or was there another one entirely? A "For those we are about to plug" one?

30

M Y DAD AND me sat in the sun at Seapoint, our backs against the wall that sheltered us from the sea breeze. When he took off his shirt, I could smell the man smell off him. Do I have a special smell myself, I wondered, a boy smell? Pulling the shirt out from my chest, I stuck my nose in and sniffed. Nothing. Nothing but the tang of the salt sea and the seaweed. Why was the sand wet? Because the sea weed. That was Jacko's joke.

Seapoint was as far as my dad would cycle after work with me on the crossbar. And only if the tide wasn't in at Booterstown or Williamstown would he come this far. He liked to work up a bit of a sweat before a swim, he said, but there was a limit. The bike wobbled as it veered across the tram tracks. Even though the trams were long gone, the tracks were still there, getting their own back on progress, especially bicycles. If you got the front wheel caught, it could send you over the handlebars with a buckled wheel. But long gone though they were, I remembered them. At least, I remembered the last tram; my dad had taken me on it the day of its final run. A double-decker it was, with the number eight on the front, and it had an arm sticking up into the air to pull itself along on its overhead wire. That wire sometimes spat sparks, and when the arm lost contact with it, then it really rained down fire.

An historic day, my dad had said it was. "For better or for worse, the trams are a thing of the past now." Sitting on his knee that day, I travelled all the way out to Dalkey and back to Nelson's Pillar on that last tram, enjoying the strangeness of it all. It was like a party. People were hopping on, going for a couple of stops and hopping off again, all the way along, calling out, goodbye now, goodbye, and patting the sides as though it was the tram they were talking to. The conductor was looking a bit weepy and not taking anyone's fare. The tram swayed and rang its bell, stopping when it met another tram going the other way, and everybody reaching out the windows to shake hands: hands that lingered as, bells clanging, the trams reluctantly pulled away from each other like twins being separated for ever.

Of the places my dad would take me for a swim on his bike, Seapoint was the best; it was better than Blackrock, just as Blackrock was better than Williamstown, and Williamstown was better than Booterstown. Sandymount, the closest, was the worst of the lot. It seemed the further you went from the city, the better the seaside got, so it wasn't surprising that to get to the really super places, you needed a car. My dad didn't have a car, but others did, and sometimes these drivers would collect us and we'd all set off on a summer weekend for one of these places. And if my dad's friend Tommy was one of the drivers, that was even better. Tommy had a car he called a Baby Austin. I wondered did baby cars grow bigger the way people did. Bit of a problem that – if their wheels grew too big for their tyres like my feet did. I'd had to get a new pair of shoes recently I'd grown so fast, and the old ones, so my dad said, hadn't even been around the block yet. Standing at the window in the last rays of the setting sun, examining the shoes, he looked like the devil. All black shadow with the edge of him red, like someone had drawn a flaming line around him with a poker.

"Lookit," the devil said. "Not a thing wrong with them."

"Not a thing," my mam, on the side of the angels, said, "except that his feet won't go near them."

"But dammit . . ."

"Dammit nothing," she said. "Do you want to turn the boy into the Hunchback of Notre Dame over a pair of shoes?" I'd seen that picture but couldn't remember what sort of shoes the hunchback had been wearing. The devil lost that round, because the next day we went to Mr Fitzgerald's shoe shop where we got a new pair of shoes on the never-never, a couple of bob a week. Mr Fitzgerald was a large man, almost too big for his tiny shop – which was made even smaller by the floor always being littered with towers of piled-up shoe boxes. He spoke quickly in a high, excitable voice that seemed to go on and on without stopping for breath as he weaved rapidly in and out and up and down the shoe-box canyons.

"They do be growing awful fast at that age missus they're just like puppies so they are his paws are growing faster than the rest of him and I have a grand pair here that I think would look well on him what size is he now a lovely shoe by Winstanley where did I put them now I just had the box in me hand sit yourself down there for a second missus I'll locate them in a minute if you can find a spot."

Tommy's Baby Austin was kept spick, and the inside always smelled like new. The padded seats squealed if you wriggled, and there were wind-down windows and little straps to hang on to for fast cornering. You could always tell which direction the Baby Austin was going to turn, because a little arrow sprang out of a slot on one side or the other to point the way. An arrow that glowed orange in the dark. In the front, besides a steering wheel that I had to stretch my arms to span, were switches, dials and knobs to beat the band. A big lever stuck up out of the floor beside the driver and went tck-tck-tck-tck-tck when you pulled on it to lock the wheels. Tommy sometimes let me control that lever. Tongue between lips and using both hands, I would work the thing like a bicycle handbrake that was on the end of the lever and move it forward to release it. Then Tommy would push in the knob with the 'C' on it, jiggle the gearstick into position and accelerate away from the curb. And if it rained, two wipers would sweep across the glass in front with a rhythm that often started a sing-song among the grown-ups. My uncle had a song about one-eyed Reilly; and my aunt had one about an eye as well, a wandering minstrel eye. But my dad's singing was the most popular. And he knew lots of songs, funny songs and sad songs and songs about the terrible things the English had done to the Irish. Everyone would say things like, good man, *maith an fear*, good on you, give us another one, when he was finished, and you could see that he was happy that people liked his singing. Sometimes he'd sing one so sad that they all got awful quiet. Then he'd sit contented, an almost-smile twitching around the corner of his mouth, taking in the silence like it was applause – a silence that was made even more so by the lonely swish and click of the wipers clearing the way through the rain for the Baby Austin.

But today wasn't raining. It was a grand sunny day, and that was massive because we were going to Brittas Bay. I was in the front of the Baby Austin and helping to drive. "You right there?" said Tommy to me. "Let her rip." I released the handbrake and we were off. But before you got under way at all, of course, there was a marvellous rigmarole that was as good as a circus. The first thing was, Tommy had to put a long handle into the front of the car and spin it to get the engine started. "Stand back now, lad, till I give her a crank." There'd be a wink to another grown-up. "You got to slide her in gently, then move her around till you get the angle just so and the rhythm right. Aha! There we go; we've found the spot. You can always tell that you've found the spot because she'll give a little shudder of anticipation."

"Tommy, would you ever mind what you're saying in front of the boy."

"What? Sure I'm only showing him how to wind up the motor, amn't I?" General good-natured tsk-tsking and upward eye movements all around. Everybody thought Tommy was great gas; he always had those around him in stitches. "Lookit here," he went on. "You've got to grip her like this and keep the thumb out of the way. That's important, because if she gets excited, she can kick back and maybe break the thumb on you. By jingo!"

The last two words were said forcefully like an incantation, as though to give him the power he needed to swing on the handle and cause the engine to roar into life. Tommy always seemed to get it in one go. Not like my dad, who never seemed to give enough swing or get the handle in the right way or something. "Ah, Jayzis, if there was hair on it you'd get it in. Here, stand back, give us a go." And Tommy would take the handle, wrap his cap around it, jiggle it into the right position, go "By jingo" as he swung and be standing there with the handle dangling from his hands, all in a flash, having churned the engine into life as easy as pie. Beaming with good-natured pride, he'd pass the handle to me. "You see what I'm saying? Develop the right touch and you'll always get results. Now, you go stow that under the back seat like a good lad."

If I could find room, that is, because divided between the cars, under the seats and in each car boot, were the other things that were needed to make the day a success: biscuit tins crammed with sandwiches; and bottles of milk; and bottles of red lemonade from Cantrell and Cochrane; and bottles of orange juice from Taylor-Keith; and Jacob's Cream Crackers; and picnic hampers with knives and forks and plates and cups; and packets of Star potato crisps, each with its own little pouch of salt rolled up inside; and a tennis ball and hurley stick to play rounders; and a tea kettle with a quarter pound of Lyon's tea and a little bag of sugar stashed in it; and a Primus stove to boil the water; and a bag of broken biscuits that my mam said were cheaper for being broken but tasted better for being cheaper; and blankets for warmth as well as for sitting on; and a tablecloth to spread on the ground; and buckets and spades for building sand castles; and a wooden crate jingling with a dozen stout for the men to have after they'd braved the waves and the rocky shore.

"Have you the corkscrew for the stout, Tommy?"

"Would you go along out o' that and teach your grandmother to suck eggs. Of course, I've got the corkscrew for the stout."

"Ah, good man, Tommy. Of course, you have."

And each youngster would have personal things wrapped up in a towel. A pair of swimming togs certainly, maybe a favourite small toy, and I always had a comb for my sea-wet hair in the middle of the tightly rolled towel. Because it had to be tightly rolled; you couldn't have the towel folded limp. Even if it took a couple of tries, you had to get it as compact and hard as though it was a football. The properly rolled towel was as much a source of pride for me as Tommy's expertise with the starting handle was for him. Which was why I never understood why Tommy didn't even bother to roll his togs in a towel at all, just stuck them into his pocket on the way to the beach, and on the drive home hung them over the outside mirror to dry.

On one trip, the bottle opener for the lemonade had been left behind, but, as luck would have it, there was a friend of Tommy's along that day who could open bottles with his teeth. As he strained at the bottle cap, people cringed and half turned away, or half covered their eyes. That way, if the bottle cap slipped and ripped his lip off, at least they'd half see it.

31

BRITTAS BAY WAS all sand dunes and tall grass for miles. You could run and jump and fall down and not hurt yourself at all, the sand was that soft. The grass was so tall, it'd hide you well when your mam was looking for you. She could be going frantic calling for you, not knowing where you'd got to, and you so close you could touch her if you wanted – but it was more fun to stay hidden and watch her squirm.

"The Prelude to the Afternoon of a Frog" was what Tommy called one of those afternoons at Brittas Bay. Disgusting was what Bermo called it. We were playing at being Nijinskys when a disturbed frog hopped out from the long grass, and me and Bermo took off after it in great, hopping, frog leaps. Thinking we had it cornered, both of us leaped toward the frog at the same time and smacked heads together so hard that I saw stars. With the hoppy hunters lying there stunned, now was the frog's chance. It sprang, landed on Bermo's forehead, hopped to his lips, then was away into the long grass. Bermo got up, spitting and wiping his mouth with his hands and going, "Yuck!" I told him he'd get warts all over his face now, and Bermo wanted to know why I didn't leap where I was looking, and who did I think I was – Jacko?

Because Jacko wasn't allowed to come on these trips. Bermo's mam said she wouldn't have a minute's peace if that misfortunate, walking calamity was along, for as sure as anything, he'd slip on a jellyfish and be swept out to sea.

Jacko sometimes came to see us off though, and then the trick was to get everything packed without giving him a chance to help. Picking up things and putting them down again in the wrong place, or dropping them all over the ground and generally getting in everyone's way was his idea of helping. One time, having been levered aside, he was standing in the road watching when somebody yelled at him to watch out; there was a van coming. So Jacko ran for safety, but he didn't look. Instead of running the short distance for the nearby footpath, he ran all the way across the road for the canal bank. With a screech of tyres and a bang, Jacko and the van made contact. Dead lucky he was that time; the whole of him could have been under the wheels instead of only his foot. As it was, he just smacked into the side of the van and was knocked flying backward with the toe of one shoe caught under the rear wheel. They took off his shoe and sock to make sure that his toes were all in working order. They were fine, wriggling away good-o like they were looking for a piano. He was brought home to his mam in tears but all right except for the bump on his forehead. "God forgive me," Bermo's mam said, "but sometimes I wish he *would* be squelched by a bus and put us out of our misery."

32

ON ONE TRIP to Brittas, one of the men brought a friend along with him. A Miss Griffith she was, who didn't seem to have a first name. At least, if she had, nobody used it. There was something stand-offish about Miss Griffith; Miss Griffith she started, and Miss Griffith she ended. She didn't smile back when you smiled at her, just looked in your direction like you weren't there. I'd become so used to being liked by grown-ups, I was puzzled. Nor was it only me; she didn't smile at any of the youngsters, like we were something catching she was afraid she might get.

Until the tennis ball got lost in the long grass, we played rounders, and then it was time for a swim. Shoes, socks, suits off. The towel around the waist so that nobody would see your mickey as you pulled down your underpants and slipped on the togs. I thought the towel ritual was pointless; the shirt-tails would serve the same purpose. Anyway, nobody would see your mickey unless they were looking, and what harm if they did? Miss Griffith must have been looking, though, because when she finally saw a bit of pink, she was scandalised and turned away with a gasp. Now, of course, they started to razz her. "Coming in for a swim, Miss Griffith?"

"No togs, Miss Griffith? Sure, I'll lend you mine when we come back. You won't mind them damp off me hot body, will you?"

And the codology only got worse when she gave her haughty head-toss. The men began talking posh and dancing together with the towels wrapped around them like dresses and then whipping them off each other. And even though they had their togs on under the towels, Miss Griffith acted shocked. "Behaving like children," she sniffed. An odd thing to say, I thought, because whatever they were doing, the men weren't behaving like children. The children were making sand castles.

"Did you hear this one, Miss Griffith?" Tommy asked, with a wink to the others. "About the posh one from Rathgar buyin' off the barrows in Moore Street. She comes to the woman with the big lip that sells the fish. She's pickin' through the fish, daintily turnin' over one after the other, and the one with the lip is gettin' exasperated. At last, when the posh wan had been there pokin' through them for about five minutes, the wan with the lip says to her, 'Listen, missus,' she says. 'They're not cocks, missus. They don't get bigger with feeling them.'"

Everybody was either laughing then or trying not to laugh. Everybody except Miss Griffith, that is. She was already stomping through the tall grass in a huff, the man she came with slipping and sliding over the sand beside her, pleading with her. He came back, grabbed his jacket and togs and said, "Jayzis, Tommy. You have me rightly snookered. Youse'll all have t'squeeze in together on the drive home because I have to take her now."

"Oh, we'll squeeze all right, never you fear," said Tommy. "You're the one won't be doin' much squeezin', I'm thinkin'."

"Jayzis, Tommy," said Miss Griffith's friend again as he ran after her up the side of a big sand dune with his shirt-tails flapping. At the top, he stopped to pour the sand out of one of his shoes, and then he was gone.

"You're a terrible man, Tommy, so you are," said my mam. "Couldn't you have left her alone?"

"What?" said Tommy. "I was only telling a joke, wasn't I?" He looked at me and winked. I wasn't sure what the joke was but wanted to stick up for Tommy.

"That's right, Mam," I said. "It was only a joke."

"That's enough out of you, now," she said. "He shouldn't be telling those jokes with you around. So you shouldn't, Tommy."

"Ah, Jayzis," Tommy said. "It was her fault, not mine. You see? That's all it takes. One good apple in the barrel . . ." Now they were all laughing again. Nobody seemed specially upset that Miss Griffith was gone. Even my mam, I knew, wasn't really cross. She was only being stern because she thought she should be, because she admitted Miss Griffith was a bit of a chore all right.

"She was more than a chore," said one of the men. "She was a right pain in the you-know-what. At least we can swim safely now. I was afraid she'd give me a cramp if she stuck around." Over the highest ridge of dunes was a beach that stretched left and right as far as you could see: straight ahead was the sea. The men charged up and over the hill, laughing and shouting down the other side as Tommy sang his song about a chicken.

In sweet Blackrock, I lost me cock. In Booterstown I found it.
In Merrion Square, I left it there, with all the girls around it.

And down across the sand they went, sand that got stonier the nearer they got to the water, then out they splashed into it until they had enough depth to dive in and swim.

Afterwards, the swimmers drew the corks from the stout bottles, the Primus was pumped up to boil water for the tea, and the sandwiches – cheese, banana, ham, egg, tomato – were trotted out. The children were told to go away and play so the grown-ups could relax. Which, I knew, meant they wanted to talk. I hovered around just within earshot, hoping to hear something interesting. Or at least get some clue as to what the you-know-what was.

33

E VEN WITHOUT A car, if you were willing to make a day of it, you could get to some good places by bike. On Sundays during the summer, with me on his crossbar, my dad and his friends might cycle out through the silent city for a picnic. Red Rock was a favourite spot. That early in the morning, you might as well be on the moon for all the people you'd meet on the streets of Dublin. All quiet except for the whirr of the bicycle wheels and the click of Sturmy Archer three-speeds changing gear, the city was all ours. Down Leeson Street, around St Stephen's Green, along Grafton Street, over the Liffey at O'Connell Bridge we'd go and head toward Howth Head with Red Rock nestled at its foot. I was too big now for the little seat on the crossbar and instead sat sideways on it, cushioned by a towel under me.

My mam, not being much of a one for bikes, never came on these trips. She didn't have a bike of her own and wasn't keen to accept lifts on them either. I had seen her on the crossbar of my dad's bike only once, and I didn't think she'd be doing it again in a hurry. Eyes screwed tight shut, knuckles white on the handlebars, she was pressed backward into my dad's chest and him shouting at her to, "Let go, let go! I can't steer. You'll have us both into the canal." They ended up in a pile on the grass with my mam's skirt so high I could see the buttons on her legs that held up her nylons.

At Sutton Cross, you turned right and followed the sea until you came to a big, iron gate beside the road. Overgrown with grass along the bottom as it was, the gate wouldn't open and had to be climbed. Lifting the bikes over it would be too much trouble, so they were always left outside. I'd slip through the bars of the gate while the rest foostered around it, and be halfway to the Martello Tower before the others even started along the path.

The hold-up at the gate was because the women were real

awkward about it. I couldn't understand why the men didn't seem to think them silly, not even with all their delaying dithering. They had to be boosted up on one side, lifted down on the other, showing a lot of leg for all of their pulling down of skirts, and they giggling and the men laughing the whole time like it was all great gas.

Beyond the Martello tower was a wood, dark and quiet and floored with pine needles, and it was at the edge of this wood, sheltered by the overhanging branches, that our camp would be set up. Those who didn't want to go swimming stayed here and got the fire going and the kettle on for when the swimmers returned. For the swimmers, a tottery climb-walk around the face of the cliff led to a horseshoe shaped cove where the water was clear and cool and deep enough, even with the tide out, for a swim.

Some of the men liked to show off a bit and, like Charles Atlases, they'd pose and strut around the rocks and dive into the deep water off the end of the horseshoe. The married men seemed to think this was unnecessary – dangerous even. Submerged, skull-splitting rocks were out there, they said, and as they had families to support, they'd walk in over the shingle, so they would, thanks all the bloody same.

Unless the woman named Cora was along. Then diving didn't seem to be so dangerous after all. Nearly all the men would be doing dives then, bellyfloppers and jackknives and high jumps out into the deep water as Cora watched and clapped and laughed, her togs leaving a wet pool under her where she sat, leaning back with one knee up and her hands stretched out behind, the bumps of her straining upward against her damp togs.

Sometimes the fun was so good around the campfire, with the songs and the jokes coming so fast, that nobody wanted to go home. Even when the songs dried up and the talk ran out, they'd continue to lie there close together in the dark, the men and the women, looking quietly into the red glow of the fire as if there was great reading and meaning in it.

If you had to go to the lav, you walked away from the fire into the wood, the black strip of your shadow leading the way. When the shadow disappeared, you knew you had gone far enough and could slip in behind a tree and do your wee flood without being seen.

Why was everyone ashamed to be seen going to the toilet? Didn't everybody have to go? Even the women? The priest said we were all made in God's image and likeness, but I didn't know about that. I had a hard time imagining God wiping his bum.

34

ONE DAY AT the grass-grown gate at Red Rock, a man cycled up and wanted to know why nobody bothered to lock their bikes. "Sure, everybody has a bike of his own," my dad said. "Why would they want to take ours?"

"That's real trusting of you, Paddy," said the man. "But I think I'll lock mine all the same." Even before he'd opened his mouth, he was pegged for an American. The clothes gave him away. Where everyone else wore natural-looking clothes in brown or black, this fellow had on blue trousers, cream socks and a jumper that was all the colours of the rainbow.

Everybody looked at each other as he fixed his bike to the gate with a lock and chain. Nobody here was named Paddy. I looked around to see had Bermo come along maybe; he was the only one I knew named Paddy. Paddy Bermingham. Not that anybody ever called him Paddy. Even his own mam called him Bermo. But later that evening, as we were on the way home, the man was running up and down outside the gate in a state. His bike, the only one that had been locked, was gone.

"Well, mister," said one of the men, "all I can say is, it must have been your expensive lock they were after."

I wanted to know who would have stolen the American man's bike, and somebody answered that maybe it was Paddy. They were still laughing when the bikes rattled over the tram tracks at Sutton Cross.

The Howth tram, the only one in Dublin that was still running, was more of a sightseeing tram than anything else, and went all the way to the top of Howth Head. From there you could see all of Dublin Bay to your right. If you looked to your left, it was rumoured that on a clear day you could see the Mountains of Mourne. There was no roof upstairs on the tram, and sometimes the clouds were that low that sitting up there was like flying. Now and again, one of the clouds would come right down and be lying across the tracks ahead, waiting for the tram. The tram would clang its bell and plough blind into it, unafraid of who it might run over. Those on the upper deck were covered instantly with a damp mist where the cloud leaked on them. I hoped any angels in there had heard the tram coming, taken their harps and flapped higher for safety.

One of the evenings at Red Rock when people were reluctant to leave, after the last of the tea was poured over the embers of the fire and we had all walked back through the starry night to the bicycles, my dad and me went off by ourselves up to the top of Howth Head. At the summit, out near the edge of the cliff among low furze bushes, I could feel the wind coming up the cliff from the sea that whispered far below.

The sea always seemed louder at night. And lonely. The whish and whoosh of the sad waves in the dark was enough to make your heart ache for you didn't know what. The stars winked at you if you stared at them for a while. *Féach, réaltaí sa spéir.* And the dark water was slashed by a yellow path to the round moon, a moon that my dad said was full of itself for having made it such a lovely night. Straight ahead, way far out, was a black line that might be England. To our right, Dublin Bay swept away in a curve, the line of street-lights reflecting in the water, leading your eye around to the clustered lights of the city in the distance.

"Look at the lighthouses," my dad said. "Down below, look, is the Baily. Your granda was in charge of that one time." The beam from the lighthouse swept the water over and over again, as though looking for something it had lost on the lonely sea.

"See that? The next one along?" went on my dad. "That's at the end of the Bull Wall. Just beyond that is the Poolbeg light. Those two, much further on and close together, are at the opening to Dún Laoghaire harbour. Beyond that we have the Muglins, off Dalkey. And look there. Way, way out on the water. That's the Kish lightship flickering out there all by its lonesome, like a lost soul on the edge of the world."

Silently I looked at the moon and the water and the sweeping lighthouses and the reflected sparkle of the curve of Dublin Bay.

Who would have thought there were so many lighthouses around Dublin? Did my granda have to cycle like mad from one to the other, I wondered, match box rattling, to make sure they all got lit on time? My dad stood behind me, his hands warm and safe on my shoulders in the chill of the night.

35

"IMAGINE, MY DEAR little boys and girls, a drop of scalding fat spluttering out of the chip pot at home on to your bare hand. Imagine the burning pain of it. Well, that burning pain is nothing compared to the fiery furnace of hell. That burning pain magnified a million times is nothing compared to the fiery furnace of hell."

The priest was preparing the class for our First Holy Communion. But before that, we had to learn about confession, because you couldn't go to communion without confessing your sins. If you did, that was another sin and you were worse off than when you started and you were doomed. I didn't want to be doomed so was listening carefully to every word the priest said. As long as you were truly sorry and confessed your sins properly, you were laughing. But you didn't want to leave it too long. You should get rid of your sins in confession regularly, before your insides turned totally black, because each sin put a black mark on your soul. Like smoking. I'd seen a big boy do that trick where you blew cigarette smoke through a white handkerchief so that it turned a dirty brown. That's what sin did to your soul: made it like a smoker's hankie. I wanted to make sure the hankie of my soul was cleaned good and proper in the laundry of confession before my First Holy Communion. I didn't want to fry for ever in a chip pot in hell.

The basic drill of the confession box seemed simple enough. When the person in front of you came out, you were to go in, close the door behind you and wait for the priest to slide open the shutter. Then you gave him a rundown of your sins, in exchange for which he gave you absolution. Now you were in a state of grace and could receive holy communion, and if you died after holy communion, you went straight to heaven. Or even if you died before it but after confession, you still went straight to heaven. If you didn't die, you had to go to confession and holy communion again and again, until you did die, for ever and ever, amen.

The problem I was having was figuring out what to confess, because how could you go to confession if you didn't have something to confess? And I had to go to confession or I couldn't go to communion, and if I didn't go to communion, I'd die roaring.

Should I confess bad words? The trouble was to know what *was* a bad word. When some people said what you thought should qualify as a bad word, it sometimes made you laugh it sounded so funny. And some people could make an ordinary word sound like a bad one. Knickers, for example. You couldn't imagine a more ordinary word. My sister wore knickers. I presumed all girls did. I heard the word all the time in our house without thinking anything of it. But one of the boys at school used to shout, "Knickers!" in a way that made it sound like a real good, juicy curse that everyone laughed at. Also, I remembered on one of my first days in school, in Low Babies, going up to the teacher to tell that the boy beside me had said a word I was sure was a bad one. Allowing the teacher to coax the word out of me, I leaned in close so that nobody else would hear me say it. "Please, miss, he said 'bum'." All of a sudden, the teacher got a bad dose of coughing and waved me back to my seat from behind her handkerchief.

Ronnie would have been great help with all of this sin stuff, venial sins and mortal-ers; he was massive at explaining things. Only he'd been carted off to hospital, and nobody was allowed in to see him.

The priest had a couple of ideas I thought I might use, though. Had I been disobedient to my parents? Well, yes, I suppose. But only if I thought they weren't listening. Had I neglected a fast-day duty? I couldn't answer that, because I didn't even know what fast days were. Unless they were the ones on the weekend. Because the ones during the week at school were certainly slow days.

Stealing. Had I ever stolen any money from my parents? No, they never left any lying around. That penny I picked up one time under the bed was finding, not stealing. But maybe a spoonful of sugar taken under the right circumstances might qualify. Mind you, my mam never told me not to take the sugar, but it would have to do. I couldn't just have the one sin, the disobedience, or it would sound like I wasn't trying hard enough. So that's what I'd do: say I stole sugar to sprinkle on my bread. Then I thought: wait a minute; that really would be a sin, to tell a lie in the confession box. So I would have another sin to tell after all. But – I was deflated again – if I confessed that I was telling a lie while I was actually telling it, then it couldn't be a lie, could it? Ah, knickers! This sin stuff was too complicated altogether. With a bit of luck, I'd die on the way to confession, and that'd solve the problem. The thing would be to be hit by a bus but not die right away, not until I was in the ambulance on the way to the I'near Hospital. That way I'd have a chance to say an Act of Perfect Contrition and go straight to heaven. So I learned the Act of Contrition inside out. But on the day, two hawk-eyed teachers, one at the front and another at the back, marched us first confessors in convoy to the chapel on St Stephen's Green. I didn't even see a bus.

36

T HE DAY OF our first confession was obviously important. We were to use the front door of the school for a change, the second time in my life I had gone down those steps into Earlsfort Terrace. Looking up at the house next door, I felt my face go hot, remembering Assumpta Jordan and her gloves. You couldn't tell from the outside that it was like a museum in there with all the stuffed animals, or that out the back was a fabulous jungle; the building looked as dull as the school from the front.

At the chapel, a tiled passageway led from the main door to two more doors inside. One door had a sign saying "sixpence", the other said, "one shilling", just like the picture house. I wondered if you could use jam jars to get in. This time we got in without paying anything. Inside, everyone was quiet and serious, communicating in whispers and sign language, if at all. On the tiled floor, each footstep clattered loudly – all the way up to heaven, I supposed. The place echoed with holiness. Was heaven an echoey place like this? Sure, that'd drive you scatty.

The confession boxes were at the back, and the class was herded in that direction to join the others already in place. There were so many first confessors that the queue spilled, fidgeting, over several rows of seats. As one sinner left his place to go into the box, the rows shuffled forward one space, like a snake creeping slowly toward its dinner. Just as I knelt down, a dazed-looking priest came out of the box and a fresh one went in. The snake slithered on.

Knees sore from gliding along on them, up one row and down another, my turn finally came and in I went. And got a shock. As soon as I closed the door, I was in pitch black. Nobody had said anything about it being dark. Stumbling forward, I tripped over a step and went down with a clatter. The prayer murmur from the priest in his stall next door stopped for a moment. I could feel the walls listening as I held my breath; the murmur started again.

Quietly I picked myself up and then realised I'd lost all sense of direction. Didn't even know which way the door was. But I'd worry about that on the way out. First I had to find the priest and get my soul cleaned. Reaching out, I felt the outline of a crucifix on the wall and knelt down to wait for the priest to finish dealing with the sensational secrets of the seven-year-old sinner on the other side of the partition.

The rattle of the shutter being opened sent me off in a rush, a bit stumble-tongued. "Bless me father for I have sinned this is my first confession I was disobedient to my parents and stole sugar from . . ." There was a cough from the priest, but it was coming from the wrong direction. It was coming from my left. Greatly flustered I turned to where, yes, I could just about make out the outline of the priest sitting on the other side of the grille. I had been telling my confession to the back wall. One of my mam's sayings popped into my mind. "I might as well be talking to the wall," she'd say. Well, I had been. And now I'd lost the thread so I'd have to start all over again. How does it go now? "Bless me sugar for I have fathered . . ."

"Yes, yes, I heard all that," said the priest. "Anything else?" I was confused. If I couldn't start from the beginning again, I was lost. I couldn't just pick up in the middle. This was like a song, or your prayers: you needed a rush at it from the beginning. Now I was in a right state. One thing I knew, I wanted to get out of here. "No," I shouted in panic. Then whispered it, "no", as if the whisper would cancel the shout I so dearly wished I hadn't let out of me. The little room was reverberating with the roar. I imagined everyone outside would be looking now and waiting for the door of the confessional to open so they could see who the screamer was, and thinking that he must be a terrible sinner altogether, and that the priest must have given him a shocking penance to make him cry out like that.

Bringing his face near the grille, the priest said, "For your penance, say three Hail Marys – quietly, my child." Then he mumbled the absolution before sliding the shutter closed, and I heard what sounded like a bit of a snigger from behind it. Let me out of here. I turned and pushed. No, no. Wrong way: this is the wall; the door is behind me. Spinning myself around, I pushed, but the door wouldn't open. I pushed again, harder. Jayzis, it's stuck. In blind panic, I stepped back as far as I could in the small space and launched myself at the door, which flew open the second my shoulder hit it and tumbled me out on to the floor of the church. It hadn't been stuck at all: I'd been pushing on the wrong side, the hinge side. Half the church seemed to be on its feet now and staring down at me, staring up, wide-eyed. Behind me, the curtains of the confession box slid open and the frowning face of the priest poked through. "I'd go easy on the sugar if I were you, my child," he said and closed the curtains again.

Among the sea of faces floating over me, featureless as balloons, I finally made out the smirking ones of Morris and Woolie. Mortified I was. So that I wouldn't have to walk through the tittering crowd, I crawled between the surrounding forest of legs. Picking myself up, red-faced, I made for a quiet pew to say my penance. Let them say what they liked. They could die roaring, the lot of them. I was in a state of grace now and ready to receive holy communion tomorrow. Or die, whichever came first.

37

FIRST HOLY COMMUNION day shone clear and sunny, and I was up and ready, first thing. My mam said the beautiful weather was a Godsend. Why wouldn't it be, I thought; wasn't this an important day for God? My mam told me not to get into the new clothes yet for fear I'd get them dirty, so in my every-day gear, I sailed down the stairs from the bedroom into the hall in one leap. My dad came up into the hall from the kitchen, a big frown on his face.

"Come here to me, you." I thought he was going to give out to me for jumping down the stairs and rattling the delft, but no. "Could you explain that to me?" he says, pointing at his bike lean-ing against the hallstand. I didn't understand what he was on about. He pointed again. "The crossbar, look at it. What's that word of yours – bockety? The crossbar is bockety. You ran into something, didn't you?"

I hadn't noticed when I put the bike back, but there was a slight upward bend in the crossbar right enough. Aw, Jayzis, he's not going to make a scene today of all days, is he? It isn't that much bent. I'd been riding the bike Jacko-style, the leg in under the crossbar, but hadn't quite managed to navigate the bend at the bottom of the lane and had hit the wall.

"Well, that's enough of that, so it is. I'm sick and tired of you mangling my bike. It's going to stop. Down to the yard with you." In fear and trembling, I did as I was told. My dad had never beaten me before, and surely he wasn't going to start today, the day of my First Holy Communion? What I saw when I went out the back door was a bike leaning against the far wall. Puzzled, I looked at my grin-ning dad. I looked back at the bike. It was too small to be a new bike for him. Could it be . . . ? My dad was nodding his head, read-ing my mind . "Yes," he said. "It's for you. A boy-sized bike that has a saddle you can reach."

I couldn't believe it. A bike of my own. "Now, be careful on it," he said. "It's not brand new, but it's the best one Christy Bird had in the shop. Look after it and it'll give you good service." Christy Bird's second-hand shop on Richmond Street sold all sorts of things – the wardrobe and the table and chairs had come from there – but I hadn't known there were useful things like bikes there. My dad carried the bike up the stairs and out the front door while I clambered after him, "thank yous" pouring out of me like a slot machine jackpot.

Outside, I gleefully examined the two-wheeled marvel which, although not quite full size, was a real bike. It had a Sturmy Archer three-speed and a back carrier, and a pump attached to the down-bar of the frame, which, of course, was black. The make was BSA; my dad said that stood for British Small Arms. It was all right for Irish small arms, too – and legs. I fitted it perfectly. Running along behind, my dad held the saddle as I wobbled down the road. A final push from him and I was sailing along Portobello Road by myself, on my very own, very first, bike. Outside Lynch's shop at the end of the road, I had to stop because I hadn't figured out the steering of the thing yet, but by lifting the crossbar under me and doing a shuffling, about-turn dance, I was able to get the bike facing the other way. Back I came, past my dad and on as far as McCarthy's at the other end of the street. I was still a bit wobbly but managed to turn properly this time and come back, teetering only a little, past my dad again, past Lynch's and on as far as the Ever Ready factory, ringing the bell like I was a fire brigade going to a blaze.

Though I tried, scooting along and flinging the leg over the saddle like the men did was beyond me at the moment. My dad said not to rush it, to take it easy, I'd soon get the hang of it, and went in to have his breakfast, looking as pleased as Punch with himself. I thought maybe I'd try the scoot and leg fling again – and came a cropper. It was a good job I didn't have the new suit on, because I ended up in the road with the bike on top of me. No damage though: a little scratch on the front mudguard was all. A scrub at my pants with lighter fluid would get out the oil mark from the chain. Just then, my mam called out that it was time to change into the new suit, and in I went, not letting her see the pants, to get all dolled up for the chapel.

The new suit and shoes were rapid. The suit was grey and went across in front of me to button on one side; the shoes were black and polished shiny like a beetle's back. My mam tucked a hankie into the breast pocket, stood back to get a good dekko at me, said I looked like Derek of the Hesperus, and slicked down my hair with a wet comb. This thing about Derek was one of her sayings. "Get the name of early rising and you can lie in bed all day," was something else she used to say. "Give a dog a bad name and hang him," was another. They made as much sense to me if they were mixed up, which I sometimes did just to aggravate her. Give a dog a bad name and you can lie in bed all day.

My dad said he wasn't quite ready to leave for the chapel yet and he'd see us there. "Make sure you do, then," said my mam sternly. "Straight to the chapel, mind. No stops on the way." Dipping her fingers into the holy-water font that was hanging on its nail inside the front door beside the spare key, she sprinkled me with holy drops before blessing herself with damp fingers. "Make sure you put on the Sunday suit," she called down to my dad in the kitchen. "And don't be late." Closing the door behind her, she took a deep breath and came out with another of her sayings: "It's a weary world we live in, and very few of us get out of it alive."

38

FTER ALL THE commotion over the confession, the communion itself was no bother. Dead easy it was: just saunter up the chapel, stick out your tongue and receive the wafer. The only thing you had to watch for was that you didn't touch Jesus Christ with your teeth, or get him stuck to the roof of your mouth so you'd have to poke at him. And you mustn't chew on him like he was a Tayto crisp, just sit quiet, teeth at ease, until he melts. Out of the corner of reverently lowered eyes, I saw Morris take the wafer from his mouth, examine it back and front, and then return it with a shrug. When asked about it later, Morris said, "I just wanted to see what a Jayzis wafer looked like, because I had me eyes closed in respect when the priest popped him in."

When it was all over, everybody traipsed out to St Stephen's Green. The mams began comparing prices of tailors and dressmakers and rosettes, because everybody had to have a whole new outfit for their First Communion. No matter what had to be done without in the months before, you were turned out smashing on that day. All the boys had new suits, shirts and shoes; a white rosette with a holy medal at the centre was pinned to the left lapel. The girls, all in white with fluffy veils, had their holy medals on a chain around their necks. Assumpta Jordan's mother was talking to Mrs Woolcott, Woolie's mam.

"Well, lookit," she said. "And I'd say it to her face if she was here." She took a quick look around to make sure her daughter was nowhere about. "That child of mine has me thoroughly vexed; had me up half the night remakin' her ruddy veil, so she had. After spendin' a fortune gettin' her the way she wanted, doesn't she see another sort of veil altogether, and nothin'll do her but she has to have the new veil or she'll die. Let me tell you, she doesn't know how close she came. I could've strangled her, so I could. She didn't want the veil attached to the plain band that really shows off her lovely face, oh no! She wanted it attached to a sort of tiara yoke that's all up and down like a bent bar of Toblerone. Sure look at her. Doesn't she look like a bleached golliwog?"

"Ah, now," said Woolie's mam. "Sure, isn't it her day?"

"O'course it is. Course it is. I only wish she'd come up with this new veil idea a week ago, that's all. Talk about a veil of tears."

A little to one side stood the men in a smoky clump, the cigarette packets being handed around to beat the band. Thanks very much. Never touch them. Well, I've just put one out, but I'll stick it behind me ear for later, thanks. The butts were being flicked away at such a rate that the shower of sparks hitting the road was like a bombardment of meteorites. Mr Mooney hawked and let a gollier out of him that landed among the butts with a splat.

"Now look what you're after doin'," said Morris's dad, with a laugh. "Some poor horse'll come along an' slip on that an' make a hames of himself, so he will."

"Don't talk to me about horses," said Mr Mooney. "With the money I'm after lashin' out here today, it'll be months before I'll be able to afford to go to another meeting."

"I was only sayin' . . ." began Morris's dad.

"Oh, yes, indeed, I'm with you there," Mr Cleary jumped in. "I could have bought me own bloody horse with the spondulicks I've put on the back of that child of mine today, so I could."

"Yes. I was only sayin' . . ." began Morris's dad again, but got no further because Mr Byrne said, "Ah now, isn't it a good thing the church gets some of your money and it doesn't all go to the bookies?"

"Lookit, don't get me started on the churches," said Mr Mulligan, gesturing dismissively in the general direction of the house of God. "Isn't that the biggest bloody horse race of the lot, huh? Answer me that! Sure, wasn't Judas only in the ha'penny place with his thirty pieces of silver, huh? They're sellin' him for a lot more these day, so they are. Inflation, no doubt."

"The thing is, I was only sayin' . . ." said Morris's dad again and, much to his surprise, got everyone's attention. Now that all eyes were turned toward him to hear what it was he was only saying, he got so flustered that he only said nothing.

"That reminds me," said my dad, and he turned to me. "Would you ever run down to the corner like a good boy and get me the *Press?*" He said to the men, "I just want to check the results." He handed over a shilling and called out to me grandly as I walked toward the paper seller. "And keep the change."

"What do you think of his new indigo suit?" Mrs Cleary was saying when I came back.

"Who are you talkin' about?" Mrs Mooney wanted to know.

"Him. The lord and master. The one who comes home after a couple a' pints of a Frida' and jumps all over me poor bones."

Mrs Byrne said, "Ah, now, Breda, you shouldn't be talkin' like that and you within spittin' distance of the church."

Mrs Byrne's spitting skills didn't seem to impress Mrs Cleary who went on, "Oh, yes. Ten foot tall he is at closin' time. Bangin' the front door behind him to announce his arrival and clompin' up the stairs lookin' for his jugglin' rights. Sure, half the time he does be asleep before he gets his pants off. In like a lion and out like a light."

I hadn't a clue what they were on about, but I did know that indigo was blue; Mr Cleary's suit was brown tweed. "What do you mean, indigo?" I asked.

"Would you listen to the young fella," said Mrs Cleary, fingering the lapel of my First Holy Communion suit. "That's a nice bit of stuff you have on. That could be your indigo suit, if you wanted. Here's the way it works. If we're stuck for a few bob, I do pawn me husband's suit. Long as I get it back in time, everythin' is game ball. When he gives me the money on payday, I goes down and gets the suit out o' hock so he can wear it for the weekend. And that's why I do call that outfit his indigo clothes: in-dey-go on Tuesda', out-dey-come on Saturda'."

Just in case she got any ideas, I gently detached her fingers from the lapel of my communion suit and took a step away. At the other side of the church door, my dad was at the centre of a bunch of laughing men, looking real happy and whipping his leg with the rolled up newspaper, as though he was a jockey way out in front on the home stretch.

Now that First Holy Communion was over and done with, we

were finished in the chapel. The only thing left to do now was go
back to the school to have the photograph taken. The teachers
lined us up in twos – boy girl, boy girl, boy girl – and said to walk
respectably in the name o' God and not make a shame of the
school. However she managed it – and I thought I'd been very vigilant – didn't Assumpta Jordan manage to get herself placed beside
me on the walk back to the school. I was livid! With the teachers
watching, there wasn't much I could do about it. But I didn't have
to be pleasant about it. To get my own back, I told her she looked
like a bleached golliwog in that veil, so she did. The jeer didn't
really work, though, because she didn't know what a golliwog was.
I made a big laugh out of the fact that she was so stupid that she
didn't even know what a golliwog was – and I'd have made an even
bigger laugh out of it if I'd known myself what it was. I stepped on
one of her white shoes and smudged it, but it didn't give me the
satisfaction I thought it should. Especially as she didn't seem to
mind that much; just gave me a haughty look and stepped on the
other one herself.

Back at the school, thirty little soul-scrubbed angels with hands
joined prayer-fashion, our class was grouped in the playground for
the photographer. A row of boys stood on a bench at the back,
with a line of girls standing in front of them; the rest of the boys
sat in front on another bench. I was on the back bench, as far away
from Assumpta Jordan as possible.

39

N OW WITH THE chapel out of the way, the best part of the day was yet to come. This was where you did the rounds of friends' and relatives' houses to show off your communion gear and everyone gave you a good-luck piece – a sixpence or a shilling maybe. Rumour had it that sometimes a two-shilling piece, or even a half-crown, might be handed over. Talk about *flaithiúil*. With a bit of luck, by the end of the day the pants would be falling off you with the silver in your pockets. I already had an encouraging bit of weight from the few bob that had been pressed on me by some of the mams at the chapel. I had taken this money with just enough polite reluctance not to seem greedy. You had to be careful with the reluctance bit – you could overplay your hand there. Timing was everything. If you went on protesting too long, you ran the risk of being believed and ending up with nothing.

My dad and I set off on our bikes, him on the outside making all the hand signals so I wouldn't have to take my hands off the handlebars of my new bike. I wasn't ready for the Tour de France yet. First stop was Lynch's shop on the corner where my dad bought ten Sweet Afton for himself, which, in spite of the name, weren't sweets; they were cigarettes. He also bought a packet of cigarettes for me which weren't cigarettes but sweets and good for a laugh. You took the sweet cigarette with its red tip out of your mouth when someone was looking and you puffed. If it was a cold morning, your breath made it look like you were puffing smoke, and some grown-up was likely to give you lacquery for smoking at your age.

Noticing the communion rosette, Mr Lynch rang up "No Sale" on the big silver till and handed over a shilling. Deadly! If everyone parted with at least that much, I'd be doing all right. The first few stops were interesting and profitable enough. Everybody made a fuss, leaning the head to one side and then the other for a good look at me like I was a piece of art, then a handbag would be foostered through, or a pocket jingled, and spondulicks handed over. After a while, though, if it hadn't been for the money, it would have been very boring. It was as though there was a very small book of things to say when someone made their First Holy Communion and they'd all read it. The women said something like, "Look at him. Doesn't he look lovely? A right young man he's getting to be." The men said something like, "B'gor, don't they grow fast? Seems like only yesterday I was all got out in me own communion suit."

At some of the houses, the bottle would be produced and a tot poured for my dad, who would say the same thing every time, like there was an even shorter book on this subject. "Ah, well, I suppose one wouldn't hurt me." If the bottle was offered again, he'd say, "Why not? Sure a bird never flew on one wing." So the day went, house after house, until I was really bushed and my dad had said, "I suppose one wouldn't hurt," a good many times and put a good many wings on a good many birds.

"A stop at your friend Scotty's," he said at last, looking flushed and happy. "Then we'll call it a day, what?" The way to Scotty's house was along Clanbrassil Street, and my dad pointed out a house to me. "Mr Bloom, the Wandering Jew, was born over there, number fifty-two," he said, as if I should know all his friends. He went into a pub for a packet of cigarettes, leaving me holding the bikes. It was much longer than the minute he said he'd be when he finally came out, carefully easing a wrapped bottle into his jacket pocket and drying his lips with his hanky.

At Scotty's, Mr Scott opened the door. "Ah, be the hokey! Is it yourself that's in it? Come on in. What's this I heard about you having a great bit of luck with the horses today?"

"Well, I won't tell you a lie, Todd, but I did. The three of them came in for me. Boys-o-boys, that was a queer bit of luck, what?"

"Fair play to you. Do you know what I'm going to tell you? You deserve it, so you do."

"And I thought I'd share some of it with yourself," said my dad, producing the bottle. "I know you like a drop of Redbreast."

"Well, now, that's very good of you indeed," said Mr Scott, clapping his hands together and rubbing them happily.

"Who is it?" Mrs Scott's voice came from somewhere behind.

"Oh, begob, her radar is workin' all right," said Mr Scott, then he called back over his shoulder, "It's the young communicant and his father, so it is." Now he took a good look at me for the first time. "Be the hokey," he said. "Don't they grow very fast?"

"Don't be talkin'," said my dad.

"It seems like only yesterday I was goin' around with me own father in me own communion suit," said Mr Scott. "And shank's mare it was. We couldn't afford bikes them days. Come in, come in. Nora," he called again as he closed the door behind us, "would y'ever bring us a couple o' glasses?"

"And one for yourself, Nora," my dad called down the hall.

Scotty and me played in the kitchen and had biscuits and lemonade while the grown-ups went into the front room and had biscuits and whiskey. Because I was nervous about leaving the new bike outside, with Scotty's help I brought both bikes into the hall for safety. The next thing, didn't Mr Scott come out of the front room and give himself a terrible whack on the shins with a pedal. I felt it was my fault for wanting the bikes in, but Scotty said it wasn't. It was because his dad was drunk and couldn't see where he was going, that was the cause of it. Then I realised my own dad must be even drunker after all the stops during the day. And we still had to get home. Opening the door to the front room, I said I wanted to leave. My dad said, "In a few minutes, son. In a few minutes." But it was much more than a few minutes when we finally set off. Now it was dark and we had no bicycle lamps. My dad said the guards wouldn't mind us not having lamps on the day of his son's First Holy Communion. His lovely son that was growing up so fast. But it wasn't the guards I was worried about. It was the motor cars, because now my dad was real wobbly on his bike and weaving over to the wrong side of the road sometimes. With a screech of brakes and tyres, a car swerved around him.

"Dad! Dad! You're on the wrong side of the road."

"No, I'm not. It's that bloody car was on the wrong side of the road."

I was crying now and wondering if we'd ever get home. "Dad! Look where you're goin'. You have no light. They can't see you. You'll be killed."

"If they were watchin' where they were goin', they'd see me all right; think there's no one else has a right to the bloody road. Ah, y' bastard." He swerved sharply out of the way of a car that was trying to avoid him and came crashing down off his bike in the middle of the street. The driver looked concerned and stopped to see if he was all right, but my dad was up and pounding on the bonnet of the car and shouting to watch where he was damn well going. Just because he had a car he thought he owned the bloody road. The concerned look on the driver's face faded: he reversed and then drove around us, shaking his head. Clumsily my dad got back on his bike and was pedalling away furiously but not getting anywhere. Through my tears, I saw that his chain was off and that's why he wasn't moving. So miserable that I didn't care about getting oil on my hands or the new suit, I made him get off the bike and took a grip of the chain. Then he grabbed the handlebars and put the weight of his foot on the pedal, jamming my fingers between the teeth of the chain wheel and the chain. I was screaming that my fingers were caught, but he was still trying to turn the pedal and calling the drivers all sorts of names. Slapping at his legs through the frame of the bicycle, I tried desperately to get his attention. Not realising what was wrong, he was now swearing at the goddamn, stupid bike and kicking downward at the pedal, and why wouldn't it turn, dammit! With my free hand, I punched out viciously and made contact. He gave a gasp and, holding his crotch, doubled over and sat down heavily. The bicycle fell on top of him with a clatter as my mangled hand came free.

Blinded by tears of pain, of fear, of anger, shame and confusion, I wrapped my lacerated, oily hand in my white hankie, grabbed my own bike and cycled away. Hoping that he *would* get run over and I'd never have to see him again, I left my drunken dad in the middle of the road, tangled up in his chainless, lampless bicycle.

40

THE SUMMER HOLIDAYS were coming, but they were coming awfully slowly. It seemed the final two weeks would never end – and then suddenly the last day of school dawned sunny and hot, like a promise of the endless summer days to come. But the minute I got to the schoolyard, I knew something was up. Everyone should've been milling round, laughing and playing, but they weren't. Even the teachers were standing in a sad bunch, not looking much like teachers at all. Assumpta Jordan came over to me slowly and with such a sorrowful face on her that I didn't even try to avoid her. Ronnie was dead, she said. At first, I thought it was her stupid try at a joke. How could Ronnie be dead? He was only seven. Only old people died. Ronnie couldn't be dead. Especially not just before his summer holidays. But I took another look at the long faces around the playground and knew it was true. Where was Ronnie supposed to go now? Because he'd been in hospital, he hadn't had his soul cleaned in confession or made his First Holy Communion. Did that mean he wouldn't get into heaven? Would he be roasted in a chip pot in hell for ever and ever?

The teachers gathered everybody around, and we all said some prayers for Ronnie's soul and then were told to go home; there'd be no school today. It seemed like an awful waste for Ronnie to die just so we could get an extra day's holiday.

I didn't think I could ever forget Ronnie, and at the beginning of the holidays I thought about him a lot. And then I thought about him only sometimes. And then not very much. I meant to, but the endless summer holidays of sun, sea, sand and canal bank made sad thoughts unthinkable. Most days were spent exploring the canal's edge, but every so often, for a bit of variety, we patrolled the nearby streets. If things were dull and we felt we needed a bit of excitement, we'd go into the Ever Ready factory yard to see if we could get a chase from the yard man. You wouldn't want to do it every day, though, because for all that he was fat, that man was fast and sometimes came awfully close to making a catch.

Scutting was another good way to pass the time. The trucks that delivered the coal had flat, open backs and were pulled by shaggy-hoofed horses with empty coal sacks across their backs in case it rained. When the driver wasn't looking, we'd rush out, grab the back of the lorry and hang there with our feet up on the rear axle. We could travel for streets like that before he realised we were there – for as long as our arms held out. One day, Jacko, Bermo and me were hanging on as the horse made his plodding way down Kingsland Parade when some sneak on the footpath warned the driver. "Scut behind, mister," yelled this informer. "Scut behind."

The driver jumped off to chase us, and for some reason the horse took this as a sign to get a move on and jerked forward. This upset a sack of coal, which tumbled a couple of big lumps of it down on top of Jacko. Luckily he got away with only a black eye and bruises all down his legs. His clothes were a sooty mess, of course. Nothing new there; he and grime were well acquainted. The driver was torn between us and the horse. The horse won. "Let that be a lesson to ye," he said, stuffing what he could of the fallen coal into his pockets before taking off after the plodding animal who, without someone on board to call a halt, might trudge all the way to Cork.

As well as the occasional trips to Brittas Bay or Silver Strand at weekends, and swimming with my dad after his work during the week, on Saturday afternoons (sometimes Sunday, too, if you played your cards right), there was the picture house to go to. The Princess Cinema in Rathmines was where we usually went. The Stella was also in Rathmines, but was posher and a little further away, and a little dearer, so the Prinner got most of our business. You lined up along the footpath for the afternoon show, watched like a hawk by Hitler, or Dracula, or whatever the usher might be called – the name changed with each new usher, even if the uniform and job didn't. The job was to patrol the line on the lookout for what he thought of as troublemakers. If he saw anyone having a bit of fun, that was all it took. He'd haul them out of the line and bar them from coming into the picture house. The rest of us he'd usher in and down to the front all together, where he'd continue to keep an eye on us from his roost at the back. Any squirming or wriggling was frowned upon and could be enough to get you flung out on your ear, though squirming was sometimes hard to avoid. Especially if we were squished two to a seat, which we would be if it was a popular picture and a lot of people wanted to see it. Then we'd all be crammed into the four rows at the front, no matter how many we were.

As well as the big picture, there might be a Looney Tunes or a Three Stooges, and there was always a follier-upper. Superman, or Clancy of the Mounties, maybe; or Roy Rogers. To be continued at this cinema next week. And the week after that. For ever and ever, amen.

So the summer went by in a slow stream of timeless, dreamy days; and then the holidays that had started out with the promise of being everlasting were suddenly galloping to a close as the dark days of September and the new school loomed. Because I wouldn't be going back to Gavan Duffy's; now that I was seven, I was too old. Now I was headed for Synge Street School.

Run by the Christian Brothers, this new school was for boys only, so at least I wouldn't have to check any more was Assumpta Jordan skulking about. That was small consolation, though. I'd willingly have traded a bit of Assumpta Jordan for some more summer holidays, because there was one thing I'd heard about this school that I dreaded. The leather. This instrument was about a foot long and constructed of several thin strips of leather sewn together to the thickness of half an inch. Laying into you with that was the Christian Brothers' favoured mode of punishment. The strips gave the flexibility needed in the execution of a really good biff across the palms of your hands. I heard some big boys boasting about taking six biffs on each hand without turning a hair. I knew my hairs would turn all right – white, probably. The only thing was to put it out of my mind so that it wouldn't spoil what was left of the holidays – if I could. But I couldn't, and it did. In happy moments along the canal bank or at the seaside or halfway through a juicy gobstopper, suddenly into my head would pop "the leather".

That'd put the moans on whatever bit of enjoyment I was in the middle of. And the closer it got to the end of the holidays, the more often the thought would come and the longer it would stay. In sheer desperation, I tried to convince myself that the real thing couldn't possibly be as bad as the dread of it, and I cajoled and coaxed and told myself not to worry. I was only wasting my time.

41

"WELL, AT LEAST Synge Street School is closer to home than Gavan Duffy's," said my dad in his well-it-could-be-worse voice, which he used only when things *couldn't* be worse. What made him think that having a school close to home was a good thing? Anyway, like it or not, the first day at the new school had arrived. Along the canal, down Kingsland Parade, along Lennox Street, around the corner and past the little house with the marble plaque on it that said George Bernard Shaw had lived there, I dragged my feet. Closer this school might be, but today it took me a lot longer to reach than Gavan Duffy's ever did. These familiar roads had never seemed so interesting before. Every house now was worthy of a slow, detailed examination. The construction of the windows, the spread of the fanlight over the doors, the way the ivy softened the lines of the brown brick walls: it was all fascinating. Finally, though, I ran out of houses and there, beyond the chapel on the other side of Harrington Street, loomed the three storeys of grey block that was Synge Street School.

The noise that was coming from the back of the school led me around the side into a jam-packed yard. I had never seen so many boys together in one place before. They were running about, making such a racket you'd think it was the start of a holiday instead of the end of one. I felt lost and was real pleased when I ran into Woolie, and I stood talking to him as though I'd rather do that than run around pushing and shoving and having a smashing time.

The noise level dropped a bit as teachers began to trickle into the yard, causing guarded interest among the boys, who examined these men curiously, wondering which one they would be getting and trying to read what sort of person he might be from his face. Some of these teachers were dressed like people and some wore the black robes of the Christian Brothers, and all started to scurry along now so as not to get wet in the drizzle that had just begun to fall. The teachers called out their class numbers as they went. My class was One B. Definny a big step up from Low Babies. A Christian Brother, black skirts flapping, roll book over his head against the rain, hurried away, calling out, "One B, follow me." I followed, leaving Woolie to start his sentence in some other part of this place.

One of the first things I learned about these teachers was that they weren't teachers; they were masters. And these masters were all men – no women here like in Gavan Duffy's. Nor were they like my dad and other men I knew who laughed and made jokes sometimes. These men all looked sour, at school anyway, because sometimes you'd see one of them on the street and he'd look like a real person, but as soon as he got near the school, on went the scowl as though it was part of the uniform, along with the grey trousers and the leather-elbowed tweed jacket. I imagined the master getting ready in the morning with the things he'd need. The red Biro and the blue Biro, the piece of chalk, and the scowl. Like my granda's teeth, the scowl would be kept in a cup beside the bed so that it would be freshly scowly for us the next day.

There were almost thirty boys in One B, and some of them stuck out more than others because of the tricks they got up to. Peter Guilfoyle, for example, could make his ears wiggle, and when he did it behind the master's back – who wouldn't know what people were sniggering at – it was even funnier. Jimmy Early made little chalices out of the silver paper from cigarette packets and could flick these little chalices, bottoms up, at the high ceiling and make them stick. Gerry Jacobs had two double-jointed thumbs that he could jerk in all directions like he was firing invisible six-shooters, his thumbs the hammers. Frankie Maher slid pins in under the skin of his fingertips so that it looked like he had a hand full of tiny porcupines. The pins he kept stuck along the top of his jacket lapel ready for when the class got dull, then they'd come out, crawl in under his skin and wave at everybody.

Ted Morrissey was called Ted the Head, because his head was so big that you wondered how he could carry it. Billy Ramsey had big ears and a funny grin and strange hair and looked like a monkey.

Eric Brown walked with his arms hanging down by his sides and slouched so that it looked like he had a hunchback. His knees were always slightly bent, as though he was ready to drop to them at any minute. The greasy head on him drooped forward so that his chin almost rested on his chest. He looked just like a letter S, so he did. And his beaky nose nearly always had a drip to the end of it which, if it did drop, would land on his knees. Fancied himself as a cycling expert, Eric Brown did. Always on about racing bikes, and special lightweight spokes, and high-pressure tyres, and twelve-speed derailleur gears, and double clangers, and quick-release cable brakes. His own bike had all those things, plus dropped handlebars. So, even as he cycled, he kept his S shape.

Then there was Freckles Farrelly, who not only looked funny – being completely covered in freckles – he sounded funny, too. His voice would sometimes go into a skid and slide over several octaves when he spoke, and he could never remember where the g's went. He'd say things like, "The butting is after fallin' off me coat." Or "Me mam uses nothin' but the best mutting when she's makin' Irish stew." And if he had to pin anything to the notice board, he used tumthacks.

The first thing we needed was the new set of schoolbooks, and they weren't cheap. My mam looked grim when she saw the list, even though you didn't have to buy new books. Second-hand was fine if you could get them, but you had to be quick. The second-hand bookstores on the Quays and along Nassau Street would be swarmed as soon as the list of books came out. Fred Hanna's, Eason's, Greene's, all of them would be picked clean if you didn't get a move on. The school blazer and the peaked cap would have to wait. "You'll get them eventually," my mam promised. "You'll just have to do without them for the moment." Because money seemed to be in shorter supply than usual these days.

The landlord was around a lot and threatening us with the law. "Give over," said my dad. "You can't get blood out of a turnip. When I get some, you'll get some." These visits from the landlord always got my dad into such a state he'd stalk out of the house for cigarettes and wouldn't come back for hours. I'd hear him fumbling at the door later with the key, and if I wasn't already in bed,

I would run up the stairs and hop into it real smart in case he started the soppy talk about school, and what a big lad I was getting to be, and how I was going to be a credit to them all, oh yes indeed. I would lie there, listening to the arguments from downstairs.

"Look at the cut of you. Where did you get the money for drink? And wouldn't you think you'd bring it home for your own children, instead of putting Larry Clarke's children through university with it?"

Or sometimes he would have brought home money that he'd won on the horses. "What do you think of that?" he'd say, sounding real proud of himself. I pictured him below in the kitchen, happily handing over a clatter of pound notes, but somehow this only made my mam more angry. I couldn't understand why. Didn't she have what she said she wanted – some money? Too little, too late and too loutish, was what she said it was.

Every so often, though, my dad would come to crackling new life, like the Frankenstein monster hit by lightning. Full of purpose and plans and promise, his rush of energy would keep him going morning, noon and night for a while. In one of these electric brainstorms, he and some other men started a printing business in a basement in Leeson Street.

Things were fine again then – for a while anyway. The rent man wasn't hammering at the door every day now, and you could answer a knock without squinting out the window first. And when I was sent out to Lynch's these days, it wasn't for a quarter pound of butter, two eggs, a cigarette and a match, oh no. It was the whole half pound of butter now, and six eggs if you please. "And a couple of rashers, me mam says, if they're not too streaky. And ten Craven A cork-tipped cigarettes, please. And a box of matches. And a pennyworth of Honey Bees."

42

ABOVE THE SOUND of my shoes clattering down the iron stairs from the street to the new printing shop in the basement, I could hear the hiss and clank of the presses as they went about their business. Full of the strange smells of paper, glue and ink, this printing shop didn't turn out books for reading out of, only books for writing in – invoice books and such. But real books must be made like this, I realised, by aproned men in basements, folding and gluing and cutting so people could read about Robin Hood or the King of the Tinkers.

The smallest of the presses wasn't electric. It was worked by foot like a sewing machine. A thing like a rolling pin collected ink from a metal plate on top and then ran down across the type. Now the inky letters would squish up against the paper that the printer had put in place. Then the printer would take it away and, as the roller re-inked the type, replace it with a fresh page; one hand in, one hand out, over and over. The scary part was when the machine was going at speed. The hands had to keep moving the whole time, in and out with the sheets of paper in rhythm with the feet. It didn't leave you time to even scratch your nose. I watched those blurred hands at their work, thinking that if they were to get out of step, they ran the risk of getting mangled in the works. The man said it wasn't that dangerous; it was as automatic as saying your prayers. You were all right as long as you didn't think about it. Or get an itchy nose.

My dad was pleased with his new importance. He was a businessman now, going about in his Sunday suit, drumming up orders – when he wasn't mucking in with his sleeves rolled up in the shop, that is. After a while, though, things began going wrong in the printing business. It seemed, according to him, the others weren't doing the job right. They seemed to think the problem was lack of orders. He said if the work was of a higher calibre, it'd be no problem filling the order book, no sir. Next thing, wasn't there a padlock on the door, and he became a commercial traveller, supplying shops with sweets and cigarettes and stuff, from the back of a red van. This job had some good points as far as I was concerned. For one thing, the van meant we could go to the seaside more often at the weekends. And sometimes a packet would burst open in the back of the van, sending sweets scattering in all directions like they were trying to escape. Naturally, those sweets couldn't be sold now, and most of them made their way into my pocket. But my dad didn't seem to think the job was all that great and was talking about going to England to get work if things didn't improve, because driving that bloody van full of sweets was a dead end, so it was. Sweets only rotted children's teeth, his own children's among them. There were more nights with him out late now and us wondering when he'd get in – and what state he'd be in when he did get in – and me holding my breath and pretending to be asleep when I heard the key scraping around the door in search of the keyhole.

Things improved, though, and the talk of England faded away when he got a job in a theatre that was behind a church on St Stephen's Green. For some reason, the plays they put on there were all in Irish. "And good plays, too," he said they were. I didn't think they could be much good if they were only in Irish, but my dad seemed to be in fine spirits with the new job. It was grand, he said, mixing with artists. He was building the scenery. "Mark my word," he said. "There'll come a time when people will be flocking in to see Irish plays, and in the Irish language, too. They won't always sneer and say it can't be any good because it's Irish. We won't be aping the English then but leading them as before. As Sheridan and Goldsmith and Wilde and Shaw did, we'll be calling the artistic tune for the English again. And I'm proud to be working in this theatre, so I am, in at the turnaround, as it were." Then he put his hands on his hips and spoke in an actory voice, "When Ireland takes her place among the nations of the earth, then, and not till then, let my epitaph be written." Winking at me, he said that maybe he should be an actor, and my mam did that thing with her eyes, like she was reading the inside of her eyelids.

Because it was close enough, I would sometimes cycle over to the theatre after school and offer to help him. But the real reason was so that I could explore the magic of painted scenery and dressing rooms and sticks of greasepaint and dark, backstage secrets. There were lamps that could give you a blazing sunset or a raging snowstorm or a flickering fire at the touch of a switch. There was a box full of broken glass that you dropped to make the sound of a crash. A big sheet of metal hanging in the dark corner gave you the sound of thunder when you shook it. Whole worlds came down on ropes from above, and in from the sides, and transformed the stage into a cabin or a cave or a mansion or a monastery.

I was there one day when the writer of one of these new Irish plays came in. I couldn't believe it; it was the man with the rumbly voice and make-up I'd seen opposite the police station on Harcourt Terrace when I was going to Gavan Duffy's. "Ah, there you are, my dear boy," he said, and the whole room seemed to vibrate with his voice. I was amazed. How could he have remembered me after all this time? But no, he hadn't. It was my dad he was talking to. But why would he call my dad a dear boy? Wasn't my dad a man? "Did you see that little domestic tiff they're putting on at the Abbey these days?" he went on. "Tragedy indeed. The Macbeths at home, more like. An embarrassment of witches is what it is."

I couldn't take my eyes off this person with the made-up face and the big hat and the flower in his buttonhole. Just upstairs might be St Stephen's Green with traffic roaring past, but it didn't seem nearly as real as this place with its spotlights and scenery and red curtains and fake thunder and mock castles. "The real world of the unreal," my dad called it.

43

I N THE LESS theatrical – though sometimes more dramatic – world of Portobello Road, things were critical once more. My dad's late nights started again, and one Friday didn't he lose his wages.

"What do you mean?" I was appalled at such a calamity, especially in these times of little money. "It fell out of your pocket, is that it?"

"Er, yes," he said, opening his jacket to demonstrate. "From here, the inside pocket. Whatever way I was cycling, I must have dropped it somewhere."

"You must indeed," said my mam almost without moving her lips, like a ventriloquist.

"What colour was the envelope?" I wanted to know.

"Er, brown. A brown envelope."

"I'll go and look for it," I said, and off I went on my bike, eyes peeled, legs and heart pumping, back over my dad's tracks, looking for the brown envelope with money in it I was sure I'd find by the side of one of the honest streets of Dublin.

The talk about England was on again. The theatre job didn't seem to be living up to expectations. I overheard some of the men talking quietly backstage behind my dad's back. They said something about the set for act three being dropped on the two-thirty at Leopardstown. And the landlord was back giving us no peace at all. My mam said her nerves were in flitters and something would have to be done. My dad said to hold her horses; something was in the works; he'd let her know. Something was in the works all right, because a morning soon after, I came down to find boxes and cases in the hall where the hallstand used to be. "Don't come home in the middle of the day," my mam told me. "I've made you a sandwich for your lunch. Eat it at school. And here, get yourself a bottle of milk." A sixpence was handed over. "And after school, you're not to come back to this house."

"Why not?"

"Just do as you're told. Go to Auntie Vera's house in Ranelagh, and don't say a word to anyone, understand?"

"Why?"

"Would you ever stop asking so many questions? We won't be living here any more, that's why. Your Auntie Vera and Uncle Joe are moving. We're taking their flat. Off you go."

I cycled to school, one hand on the handlebars, examining the coin I'd been given. Even though this was Ireland, it was an English tanner with a lion standing on a crown on one side and the head of an English king on the other. Well, English or not, there didn't seem to be any reason to waste it on a bottle of milk. The toffee man came around the school on his three-wheeled bike that was like an ice-cream cart, only there was broken toffee in the front compartment instead of ice cream. I decided I could buy a bag of toffee and still have money left out of the tanner for Nancy Balls, maybe.

After school, forgetting I'd been told not to, I went back to Portobello Road, gnawing on the last of the toffee, getting rid of the evidence. At first, I thought there was a fire or something, because there was such a crowd around our house when I got there. Then I remembered it wasn't our house any more. The landlord, using his hands as blinkers, was moving his face around the front window like he was one of them sucker fish. The bunch of women gathered around didn't seem to know anything about our family when they were asked. Scarcely even knew our names, it seemed. "Ah, no. No idea. Sure, I rarely spoke to them. Hardly knew them. Haven't a clue where they might have gone."

When Bermo's mam saw me, she waved me on urgently, like she was a policeman on point duty and I was holding up traffic. I twigged what she meant and shot off before the landlord saw me. It hadn't sunk in when I saw the stuff piled in the hall in the morning, but now the finality of it hit home. I'd never be coming back to this house again. No more jumping down to the hall from the bedroom, or playing on the canal bank, or fishing for pinkeens among the reeds. I'd have to come a long way now to laugh at Jacko falling into the jayzis canal.

Over the canal bridge and along Rathmines Road I cycled until I came to Rathmines Church, where I cut through its grounds and out the back gate. Around Mountpleasant Square now and on to Ranelagh Road and under the railway bridge beside the Little Sisters of the Poor and passed Gilbey's Wine Merchant and the Lucan Dairy and the public toilets at the Triangle, I pedalled. It was like the bike knew the way, because I wasn't minding where I was going.

I told myself I was lucky; Auntie Vera's house was a lot bigger than the house on the canal. A much better place to live altogether. But I couldn't understand why I had such a lump in my throat. The new house was just ahead, but I was having a hard time seeing it because of the rain streaming down my face. Funny thing, though, the roads were dry.

44

THE WORD AMEN means so be it, half-a-crown and a thru-penny bit, two men, four feet, walking down O'Connell Street. Portobello Road was in the past; Ranelagh was where we lived now, in a flat on the main road over a shop belonging to the Dartry Dye Works. So be it.

Up! This house was all up. Up stairs that turned back on themselves at landings at the back of the house and again at the front. Up from the hall to the kitchen. Up more stairs to the sitting room. Up again to where there were a couple of bedrooms and the unbelievable luxury of an indoor toilet. Finally some more stairs took you to the very top of the house where the biggest bedroom covered just about the whole of that floor. The ceiling here sloped sharply down on the front of the house and had a built-out window with a sill deep enough to climb comfortably on to. Doing your best not to step on any breakables, you went over the top of the dressing-table mirror and there you were, close to the sky. By tilting the window dangerously open, you could see up and down the main road. This great height was exciting, as much for the danger as for the view, because one slip and you'd be a goner. You'd go skidding down the steep slope of the slates and wouldn't stop until you reached the busy main road far below. It wouldn't matter whether you were run over by a bus then or not, because the fall would be sure to have killed you. To the left was a view as far as the Sandford Cinema. To the right you could see all the way to the Triangle and the road to Rathmines. Off in the distance, beyond the roof of Gordon's, the ironmongers, loomed the green dome of Rathmines Church. From this window, you had a great view of the sun going down in ruby genuflection behind that dome on summer evenings.

My mam said she missed the Portobello Road neighbours, and I certainly missed the canal bank and Bermo and Jacko. But

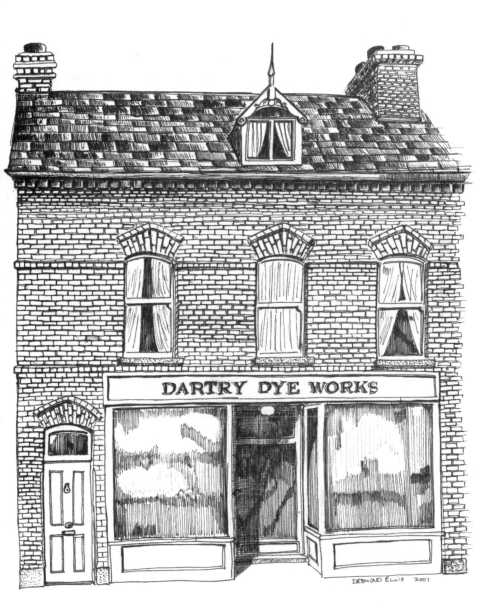

DARTRY DYE WORKS

DESMOND ELLIS 2001

getting used to the new house and the surroundings kept me occupied. There were new streets and laneways and lots of shops on both sides of the street to explore. My dad was interested in the shops too; certainly Humphreys Public House across the road might come in handy, he said with a smile. My mam, without a smile, said she thought it might be maybe too handy. All in all, though, she seemed to be pleased enough with the new arrangement. For one thing, she said, washday would be so much easier now with the help of the geezer in the bathroom. I thought she meant there was some oul' fella in there to help her wind the sheets dry, but it was a big boiler she was talking about, with a lid on top and a spout you could swing out over the bath to fill it. And it was a real bath, not a tin tub; a real bath that you could lie down in. All my mam had to do was light the gas under the geezer to heat the water when someone wanted a bath. Or to do a wash, she lifted the lid on the geezer, popped the clothes in and, as they merrily bubbled their stains away, just gave them a stir from time to time, like she was making soup.

And having an indoor toilet was deadly. No more traipsing out to the end of a freezing yard in the winter. And the fact that the toilet wasn't in the bathroom but upstairs on the next floor was always good for a laugh. Polite people asking for the bathroom always came back with a puzzled look on their faces and a "No, I mean the, em . . . you know."

"Oh, you mean the toilet? It's upstairs." A long chain dangled from a water tank high up on the wall above the toilet. Pull this chain, and in a jiffy, all your gic is in the Liffey.

And the sleeping arrangements couldn't be better. Because I was the eldest, I got to have a bedroom of my own. And those who had come between me and the window in Portobello Road – the sister, then the brother, then the other brother – were out of sight now, all of them together in the top bedroom. My room might be the smallest of the lot, but it was private, with a door that I could close on the world.

The first room you met on the way up from the hall was the kitchen, which quickly became the centre of operations. In no time, it took on the hues and smells of our old house and filled up with the familiar clouds of steam. Soon the table looked just as it had, with the most-often-used things gathered in a jumble in the middle of it. The loaf from Johnson Mooney and O'Brien sat on its round cutting board in the centre, with the bread knife and the Galtee cheese close by. Radiating out from the board, like planets around the sun, were the other frequently needed spreads and things: Coleman's mustard made in an egg cup, its apostle spoon standing up in it ready to perform a miracle on a thin slice of ham; the sugar bowl; the tin of Lyle's Golden Syrup; the bottle of HP sauce; salt; pepper; butter; Golliwog marmalade; the box of Corn Flakes; and often the morning's ripped-open bills propped against the bottle of milk to be scowled at by my dad when he came home. What was the point of putting things away if you were only going to be taking them out again in a short time? In any case, the places they came from originally had been taken over long ago by other things. The bread bin now held the insurance books and the brown paper bags that were saved to be used as lunch bags. The canister for the sugar was given over to the books of Green Shield Stamps that were being saved up for an alarm clock.

Cooking was easier now, too. No more fussing with coal and sticks and papers for the range these days. Now there was a gas cooker with four burners, an oven below and, above it all, a fold-down rack for warming the plates. Not that plates were ever warmed there, but it was a dandy place to pile the most-often-used pots and pans. As long as she had a couple of pennies to put in the gas meter, all my mam had to do was light a match and turn a knob.

The knob for the oven was different from the others. This one was hinged so that it hung down, and you had to lift it up into position before you could turn it. I was mucking about with it one time and it broke off in my hand. No one saw, so I stuck it back in its slot and left it for someone else to break. Later I heard my sister scream from the kitchen and I rushed in to blame her, but by the time I got there to confront her, can you believe it, she was so sneaky she'd stuck the thing back together again for somebody else to break. To turn the oven on now, my mam had to stick a penny in between two little prongs like a bird's beak, all that was left of the knob, and twist. A turning-on penny was always left on the mantelpiece for this purpose. You could have used a half-crown, of course, if you had such a thing.

"Hey, Mam," I asked, "will we get a new gas cooker if we win the Sweep?"

"We will not," she said. "What I'll do, though, is leave a stack of half-crowns on the mantelpiece for turning on this one."

To keep the gas flowing, pennies had to be fed into a meter in the cubbyhole at the end of the hallway downstairs. You could have built a spaceship with what you might find in that cubbyhole. Thrown together higgledy-piggledy were nails, screws, hinges, hammers, unrecognisable bits from things long lost, doorknobs, chisels, toothless saws, keyless locks, rusting files, bits of flex, cracked picture frames, half-full cans of paint, half-empty jars of turpentine, shoe lasts, scraps of leather that might come in useful someday and a headless Child of Prague, waiting patiently for his glue. There were other things – lamps, toys, electric irons – that might, maybe, possibly, get fixed sometime in the future if my dad could find time to get around to it, and didn't, while he was about it, break another tool that would join the ever-growing legion of the lost in the depths of the cubbyhole.

45

I HAD A greater distance to travel to school now, and this meant an earlier start in the mornings. If I'd left it too late to walk – I wasn't ready to go on the bike yet, not with the morning traffic roaring through Ranelagh – I'd have to take a bus. Except you couldn't always count on the buses. There'd be none at all for a while, and then a whole clatter of them would all come along at the same time, as though they were afraid to be out on the streets by themselves. When my mam went to buy a bus guide so she'd know the times the buses were supposed to show up, the lady behind the counter laughed. "Jayzis, missus," she said, "you're a bit old to be believin' in fairy stories, aren't ya?"

Often, having no great desire to be in school in the first place, I lay in bed as long as I could in the morning, which meant me running after the bus with my mouth full of toast and my coat half on. And, of course, in the wintertime, in your knitted gloves, if you made a running grab at the bar at the back of the bus, you were likely to swing yourself right around and off the bus again. You never expected the bus to stop for you when the driver saw you running, of course, but in the unlikely event that it did actually stop, this wasn't necessarily a good thing. It'd throw your timing off and you'd maybe smack your shins against the edge of the platform, pitch forward, and end up sitting at the bus conductor's feet. Never mind that you might have two broken legs, he'd always try and be funny. "Get up off yer knees. Mass is over," he'd say. Or "Did ya have a nice trip?" And once, "How's it goin', Nijinsky?" Then, ding-ding, he'd go on the bell to set the bus in motion again.

The upper deck of the bus had the best view, especially if you got the front seat. It was also where the smokers went. In the crowded mornings, you could maybe see out the window and across the street, but you wouldn't be able see across the aisle with the clouds of smoke. Like an opium den it was. That figure looming at you out of the fumes might not be the conductor coming for his fare; it could be Fu Man Chu coming to cut your throat.

Being late into Synge Street School in the morning was frowned on. Let it happen too often and you were a likely candidate for the leather. That foot-long, flexible implement of torture hurt something awful if you got a biff with it. And some of them, the serious biffers, really laid into you. They'd take a couple of warming-up practice swings through the air before they were ready to go for your extended hand, which they had to twist and turn to get at the correct angle first. They could take minutes lining up the shot, like they were playing conkers and you were the chestnut. And woe betide you if they made you so nervous that you pulled your hand away at the last minute and they missed. Now they were really angry, because they'd been made to look dopey in front of a class of tittering schoolboys.

"You there, Cunningham. You sniggering? At me, maybe? Yes, you are. Out to the line. I'll give you something to snigger about. I'll warm your hands next."

The thing was, you were always so nervous of the biffers that you were sure to do something wrong in their class. You never knocked over your bottle of Stephens blue-black washable ink in a non-biffer's class. You could go all day, dipping and writing, and not a blot nor bother on you. But, in a biffer's class, you were that nervous that your pen got to be the size of a pickaxe and your elbows became two boiled hams. Six of the best on each hand was what you got for knocking over a bottle of ink. And it wasn't even the school's ink. You had to bring in your own bottle of ink to spill.

Nor was punishment necessarily dispensed right away. You might be made to stand on the line for hours first. Instead of biffing as they went, some of them would save it all up till the end of the class and make a meal of it. That was much worse than getting the biff there and then, because the anticipation seemed to make your hands softer or something. Sometimes there'd be that many out at the line waiting, you'd think he couldn't possibly get through everyone. You'd pray then like you'd never prayed before that, please God and his Blessed Mother, the master would die before he got to you – or at least have a paralysing heart attack.

And some boys spent more time out on the line than others. Not that they were necessarily more deserving or anything, but they just seemed to attract the leather like magnets. Just as boys like Jacko were always walking into things, so others got biffed a lot. I was lucky; I wasn't a magnet. Poor Freckles Farrelly was, though. The masters were never quite sure that he wasn't being funny with his "mutting" and his "buttings", so they'd often biff him just in case he was being cheeky.

Spitting on your hand before the biff was supposed to lessen the effect. Others believed that rubbing your palms back and forth real fast on the front of your trousers would do the trick. But whatever it was you tried before the biff, afterward was always the same: the hands tight in under the arms to cut off the pain; the eyes clamped closed to hold in the tears; the mind shut down so as not to think about the humiliation.

46

THERE WERE FOUR Dalton brothers, and they lived around the corner from me on Sallymount Avenue. All of them went to Synge Street School and Ciaran, the youngest, was in my class. Awfully embarrassing to be with, he was always talking about God and trying to sound holy in such a loud voice that everyone on the bus could hear him. Did he think God was deaf? He'd come out with something like, "What would you rather be, the lick of a cat or the prod of a pin?" As though nobody would know that the lick of a cat was supposed to be a Catholic and the prod of a pin a Protestant. Me squirming with the whole upstairs of the forty-four bus listening. If only I'd been smart enough to say, "Neither, I'd rather be a heavy dew and I'd fall on you."

The Daltons went to mass and holy communion every morning. Ciaran announced this to the class one day by way of showing off. If he felt that everyone would be in awe at the holiness of him, he was wrong-shipped there; instead, we accused the Daltons of being greedy buggers that wouldn't leave a bit of communion for anyone else. If we all died roaring, we said, and went to hell for the want of a wafer, it would be because the Daltons had snaffled all the holy communion in Dublin.

And then there was the Daltons' mam. Where other mams might make a sheriff's badge for you out of a cardboard star covered with silver paper, or a pirate's hat out of one of their scarves, what would the Daltons' mam be making for them? Priest's vestments! While me and my friends were out in God's fresh air, playing cowboys and Indians, the Daltons would be stuck inside in the devil's gloom, playing at saying mass in crepe-paper vestments with cardboard communion in tinfoil-covered teacup chalices. All going to be priests, the Daltons were. No surprise there. The oldest one was halfway there already. "And, please God now," Ciaran said, "in a few years' time, he'll be out in Africa, converting the heathen black babies."

Jimmy Earle whispered, "Please God now, youse'll all be eaten by the heathen black babies."

The Christian Brothers seemed to be very interested in the black babies. One time, they had us all collecting the silver-paper caps off the milk bottles for the black babies. What the black babies wanted with them I couldn't figure out. Did they perhaps use them as money? If that was the case, maybe I should collect my own bottle caps and go to the country of the black babies where I'd be a millionaire. Another time it was a card with a rosary printed on it that the Christian Brothers handed out. You could sell each bead on the card for a penny, and whoever gave you the penny got to poke a pin through the bead. When all the beads had been poked, you gave the card back to the Christian Brother, along with the pennies. You could keep the pin. Of course, that put paid to my theory of becoming a milk-cap millionaire if the black babies were also collecting pennies. Maybe I should ask one of the Daltons to find out for me when the eldest brother got out there among them.

Naturally, the Daltons were all altar boys. Ciaran went one better by also singing in a choir. Always annoying me to become an altar boy, he was, saying how it would be good for my soul and help me make a happy death. I wasn't even nine yet, and it was a happy life I was after right now, thanks very much. Besides, I never really knew what was going on at mass. Sit down. Stand up. Bless yourself. Genuflect. Bow your head. So as not to make an eejit of myself, I always sat back a bit in the chapel so I could copy what the people in front of me did. But just to shut Ciaran up and stop from being cross-examined in front of everyone on the bus, I finally agreed to join the choir – which turned out to be not too bad a move. Once a month, Mr Mortimer, the choirmaster, gave out bus fare for every time you showed up. Tuesday and Thursday evening for practice and Sunday for mass – it mounted up. And, as I usually rode my bike, it was like found money, free, gratis and for nothing. One Sunday, though, I was sorry I didn't know more of what went on during mass. That was the morning I was sent out to the loft to watch the mass and was to call the choir from the back room when it was time for them to come out and sing.

Out there by myself, I hadn't a notion what to look for. Perhaps I'd recognise something, get a clue, if I watched intently enough. I might as well have been staring into a bush. Yes, here was a bit I recognised. Sanctus, Sanctus, Sanctus, where the little bell – like a bicycle bell – rang three times. But should the choir be here by now or not? I wasn't sure. Now, here was something I'd never seen before. The priest turned around, looked up at the choir and shrugged his shoulders. But maybe he always did that and I just never noticed. So I continued to sit there, waiting for something, anything, to happen.

Something did. A choirboy came from the back room for a look, muttered a word I didn't think should be said in a chapel, and went clattering out again. The others all came running now, tumbling, stumbling to get into place. Mr Mortimer leaped for his bench and, before he'd even stopped sliding, was pounding on the organ, hitting the keys with such force that the priest on the altar shot his head down between his shoulders like he was a tortoise. The altar boy who was swinging the incense took advantage of the confusion to get in a complete over-the-head-circle with the smoking pot. I felt like a right eejit altogether.

I liked the choir loft, though. Up there above everyone else, we sat in front of the big organ pipes like we were angels looking down from on high. Although angels isn't what would come to mind if you saw the goings-on sometimes. Comics were known to be read there from time to time during the mass. And the wide, bum-polished, wooden benches were ideal for a sneaky game of shove ha'penny, between hymns.

Easter was impressive. Everybody brought to the chapel a candle that had been blessed by the Holy Father himself. At a certain moment, all the lights went out and everything was dark and quiet, not even a prayer cough. A flash came from the altar as the priest lit his candle. All you could see from up where we were was that one lone little flame in the vast, dark space: a tiny lighthouse in the gloom. Then it moved toward the altar rail and lit the first candle in the first row. The two lights flickered close together for a second as though they were whispering to each other, and then one of them leaned over and told the next candle to wake up.

Each candle in turn tilted over, passing the flame on, candle to candle to candle. Gradually the place brightened as the trickle of light became a river of flame that poured down one row and back along another, from the front to the back, until the whole chapel was filled with a gentle glow. Hundreds of tiny lighthouses to guide you safely home.

47

ART TAKES YOU out of yourself. That's what Brother Devoy, the art master, said. It certainly took you out of your usual classroom. Because of the need of storage space for paper and paint and brushes, and running water and a sink for cleaning up, you had to go to another room for the art class. This room was on the school's top storey, and to get to it you went up iron steps on the outside of the building. From the top step, the Christian Brothers below were like large crows scuttling about, arms folded behind their black backs like wings, looking for some poor worm of a schoolboy to pick on. You could also see the wasteland over the fence where the rest of the houses on the street had been knocked down to make way for the new school. All the houses on Synge Street between the school and Grantham Street were gone like a bomb had hit them. I thought there was something wrong with that, putting people out of their houses just to build a school.

Digging had already started on the foundations, and it all looked bleak and depressing. With muddy-water-filled holes and trenches, it looked more like the end of a war than the start of a new school. Brother Devoy said these trenches with their parallel sides were a good example of what he had been teaching us, vanishing points and perspective. Where the sides and the bottom all come together in the distance was your vanishing point. Same with Synge Street outside, he said. Look along its undemolished side and you'd see that all the houses and railings and footpaths had all converged and shrunk down to a dot.

"Sir, sir," said Gerry Scully. "I have a drawing for you of all the streets in the world." He handed over a blank sheet of drawing paper. "That's all their vanishing points, sir."

"That's very clever, Scully," said Brother Devoy. "Now I'm going to make you vanish. Go and stand outside the door for a while. Maybe that'll put things into perspective for you."

If you were to go to the end of the road in search of the vanishing point, it wouldn't be there any more. Somehow it would have snuck around behind you and be back where you came from, and you'd be standing on somebody else's vanishing point. Trying to find out where a vanishing point had gone was like trying to find a bunghole without a barrel. I figured, as vanishing points didn't really exist, we were spending all this time learning about nothing, yet Brother Devoy still rattled on as though it all made perfect sense, as though he had a pocketful of vanishing points he'd hand out at the end of the day to everyone who did well in class. A vanishing point caused perspective. Or maybe it was the other way round. Anyway, one of them, or both of them, made things disappear. It only worked in art though, more's the pity. Sometimes, when I would be on about how awful school was, some grown-up would say, "It can't be that bad. Let's put things into perspective." How I wished I could, and make the school, the masters and the leathers all just vanish into a squished point.

The school year snailed along, and when the summer holidays finally came, I spent a couple of weeks delivering for Miss Crawley in the laundry downstairs. It was dangerous work. With its little wheel and big basket full of laundry on the front, the bike was very top heavy and unbalanced. For safety's sake, you were better off not touching the brakes at all, but trying to stop without brakes could be just as dangerous. I'd try to time it so that I'd stop pedalling the proper distance away to coast to my stop. And if I misjudged and went past it so that I had to turn and walk back, pushing the cumbersome yoke, that was fine by me.

My job was to take the freshly washed bundle to the customers and bring back whatever they had that needed washing. Then it would be sent on to the laundry at Dartry and be brought back to the shop for me to deliver when it was done. On one trip, I misread Miss Crawley's scrawly handwriting on the bill and delivered the laundry to the wrong address. The right address phoned the shop later, looking for their sheets, pillowcases and tablecloths, and I was sent out to undo the damage. The man I'd given the bundle to in the first place opened the door, and I explained the problem. He said that, presuming it was hers, he'd given it to Miss Gillespie in the flat upstairs just as she was going out, and she had put it on the chair inside the door, locked up and left. I must have looked like the end of the world had come, because he said, "Don't worry. Tell you what. I'll get a ladder. Her window's open; you can climb up and get your parcel."

Tongue sticking out, I climbed in wobbly fashion to the open window – and got a shock. Miss Gillespie must have come back again, because she was inside and had almost no clothes on. I slid down the ladder so fast the friction burned my hands. My face, too, was burning as I tried to explain to the man holding the ladder what had caused my rapid descent. I must have been gulping too much air, because he decided the problem was I had no head for heights, told me to take a deep breath and went up himself. It took him a lot longer to come back down the ladder than it had taken me, and he had a big grin on his face when at last he did come down.

"I had to wait till she got out of the way and I could see the chair," he explained. "The laundry's still there. I'll go up and get it for you now."

When he came back with the bundle of laundry, the grin was still on his face. He gave me a shilling and told me to bring my spare laundry here any time I felt like it.

48

WOOLIE AND I were classmates again in Jumbo Doyle's class when the next school year began. Jumbo was a large man with a large nose and he looked like that French general, De Gaulle. Always nattily dressed and smelling of aftershave, Jumbo wore lace-up boots and had a crease in his pants that could cut butter – and he thought he was funny. Nothing he liked better than to come along behind you as you sat at your desk and grab you by the short hair in front of your ear and pull you right up out of your seat with his finger and thumb. Woolie was a favourite target. "Aha!" he'd say as he hauled him, squirming, upward. "Woolgathering again, are we, Mr Woolcott?" And he'd cackle as though he'd said something comical.

Or if he caught anyone eating sweets in class, he'd take the sweets from them and eat them himself. You'd watch the lid of his tall desk being raised at intervals as another sweet was transferred from the stolen bag to Jumbo's mouth. Then, at the end of the day, he'd give back the empty bag. When he caught me having a sneaky word with the boy beside me, he hauled me up to the front of the class by the ear and gave me two biffs on each hand. "This mightn't make you clever," he said with his stupid cackle, "but it definitely will make you smart."

Every so often, my mam would take a look at me, come out with her saying about me looking like Derek of the Hesperus, and give me the money to get a haircut on the way home from school. "Either that, or buy a fiddle," my dad would say with a laugh.

The barber's shop was on Camden Street, and one day when I got there, a couple of men were already sitting around waiting, so I sat down with them to wait for one of the two barbers to get to me. What with the big window and the mirrors and the white walls, it was very bright in the shop. And, whenever a double-decker bus went by, the sun reflected off the bus's upstairs windows and into

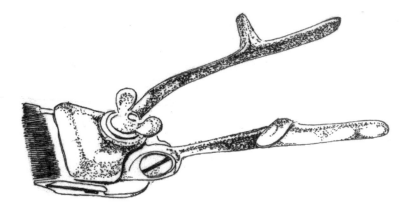

the barber's, where it flashed blindingly through the jars of Brilliantine hair oil lining the window shelf and made golden beams chase after one another around the walls.

In the middle of the floor sat three hefty barber's chairs in a row. These chairs could be made go up and down, swivel and tilt by the barbers working pedals and levers on them. One of the chairs was already tilted all the way back, with a man stretched out on it waiting for a shave. Head wrapped in towels like a mummy, only his nose showing, he dozed like a cat in the sun.

At another chair, a man was being worked on by one of the barbers with a straight razor. The barber's left hand was holding the man's nose. The right hand – little finger in the air – started each razor stroke slowly; carefully rasping over the soapy stubble on the chin; it finished with an upward flourish of the razor as if the barber was conducting an orchestra. Wiped clean on a piece of white paper that was on the man's shoulder, the razor was ready again to scythe through some more stubble.

In the meantime, the second barber was giving a haircut to a man in the last chair. Around the back of the man's neck he went with a pair of clippers that was like a little lawnmower. Clip-clip-clip, his hand mowed, and the hair tumbled away down the back of the chair to the floor. As the scrawny neck of him became bit by bit revealed, the man began to look like nothing so much as a chicken being plucked.

Finished with the mowing, the barber next whipped a small scissors from his top pocket and snipped the tufts of hair sticking out of the man's ears and nose. Now a little sweeping brush whisked away any loitering loose hairs from around the shoulders and the back of the neck, and the man's head was ready for the next step. Sprinkling hair oil into his hand from a bottle like the vinegar bottle in the chipper, the barber rubbed his palms together to get them good and slimy. The man in the chair was admiring himself in the mirror and humming a little song to himself as he was oiled and slicked down until his head was shiny black like a skating rink.

"You've got a voice like an angel, so y'have," said the barber, running a comb through the oil slick. "Hark, the hair-oiled angels sing."

When he'd washed his hands free of oil, the barber started slapping a big cutthroat razor backward and forward along a strap hanging from the wall beside the mummy still stretched out in the first chair. Catching my eye in the mirror, he asked, "How was school t'day, young lad?"

I made a face. "Terrible," I said.

"Why is that?" asked the barber. "Sure, isn't y'school days the best days'f y'life?"

"No, they're not," I said. "They're terrible. I got biffed today – for nothin'."

"Don't believe that, y'must've deserved it." The barber was whipping up a dollop of soapsuds in a little cup.

"No I didn't. It's just that Jumbo Doyle is an oul' bags."

The barbers straightened up a little and caught each other's eyes in the mirror. What was wrong? The mummy lying back in the chair cleared its throat and uncrossed its legs. The uncrossing of the legs drew my attention to the boots. The highly polished, brown, lace-up boots and the cuffs of the well-creased trousers. Jumbo Doyle! I was out of that shop like a flash. I cursed myself. I should've known; the big nose sticking up out of the wrapped towels should have been the giveaway. I went home that day without a haircut – or a fiddle.

49

FROM THE CLASSROOM window, I watched the walls of the new school rising upward, a little more every day. High overhead, heavy loads swung alarmingly from a crane that looked no more substantial than an oversized Meccano set. Shouting men ran up and down ladders and along scaffolding, carrying bricks and planks and copper pipes and coils of wire. When the windows were in and plastering finished, the scaffolding came down. When the big double doors at the front went in, the electricians and the carpenters and the plumbers and the tilers arrived to put the finishing touches to the inside. When all that was done, they closed up their tool boxes, strapped them to the back of their bicycles and cycled away.

The school was opened with a big celebration of politicians and speeches and banners and bishops and Christian Brothers and holy-water blessings and photographs. Not that I was actually looking forward to it, but having watched it grow from a hole in the ground, I was curious to see what the inside looked like, and when the day finally came, we piled in, clattering and snooping, through the orderly, echoey newness of it all. I had the feeling the Brothers didn't really want to let us in – as if they felt we'd spoil it somehow. But, of course, they had to, because a school without pupils would be like the canal without pinkeens: unimaginable.

Unlike the gloomy, poky rooms of the old school, the new schoolrooms were big and bright and clean, so I suppose this was an improvement. From their quiet conversations together, though, it seemed some of the masters preferred the old place. I heard them talking about the sterility and lack of character in the new school. Sure, the old school was all dark wood in dim rooms with gloomy corners and narrow stairways. If that's what character was, leaving it out of the new school was the right thing to do. This place was clean, unspoiled, with no bad memories lurking anywhere.

There was even sunlight in this new school. Small specks of dust –
characterless dust, no doubt – frolicked in bright sun shafts like
angels looking for the head of a pin to dance on. Although why
angels would want to dance squished together on the head of a pin,
I could never understand. Being angels, couldn't they dance where
they liked, in the very best places? The Metropole if they fancied.

The blackboards here were unbelievably huge. Fixed to the
walls, they slid behind and in front of one another like the glass
case at the butcher's. No more awkward easels with the board balanced on them, that took up so much space and looked like they
might fall down any minute but, more's the pity, never did. And
for all that they were called blackboards, these new sliding things
weren't black at all but green. Easier on the eyes, they said, as
though the colour would make doing sums any easier on the eyes.
The desks of pale-coloured wood were brand new and uncarved.
Young hands moved over the smooth surfaces like so many
Michelangelos caressing blocks of marble.

I got my hopes up when I found out that Brother Devoy was to
be the headmaster of the new school. An artistic headmaster might
change things for the better. Surely he of all people would know
that biffing could ruin a budding artist's hands. Maybe the leathers
would all be banned now and woven together into one large piece
of expressionistic art that would sit in the front hall as a tribute to
the schoolboys who'd toiled here in the dark ages before this new,
biff-less age of enlightenment. I was dreaming in Technicolor; it
didn't work out that way at all. Perhaps an art master's perspective
changes when he becomes headmaster, because not only did the
day-to-day classes become no better, but there weren't even any
more art classes. Oh, Brother Devoy would come into the classroom from time to time to see how things were, or give a little talk
about health maybe, or share some hints on how to save your
immortal soul, but vanishing points and perspective, it seemed,
had no place within the clean and parallel walls of the new school,
and they were never mentioned again.

On one of his visits, Brother Devoy told us about something that
might save not only your soul, but your life as well. Scapulars he was
talking about, blessed strips of cloth that went over your shoulders

and hung down front and back under your shirt with a holy medal or a relic or something sewn into the pouch where the two strips joined together.

It seems there was a priest one time, so Brother Devoy said, who forgot to put on his scapulars one winter's morning. Off he trudged through the freezing rain on his way to say mass, and it was only when he reached the chapel that he realised he wasn't wearing his scapulars. Should he traipse back through the cold damp to get them? He decided he should and finally got back again to the chapel, tired and wet and cold. But, in the middle of him saying the mass, didn't a madman jump up and shoot the priest in the back. This was in America somewhere. But the priest didn't fall and went on with the mass when the man was taken away. Afterward, the priest took off his chasuble. There was a bullet hole in it. He took off the alb. There was a bullet hole in that, too. There was a bullet hole in the amice. There was a bullet hole in the priest's shirt. There was a bullet hole in his vest. And there in his scapulars, didn't they find the bullet, squashed flat. We all put our names down for scapulars right away – even though we might never go to America.

I wondered if the Daltons knew about these scapulars. It might keep them from being eaten alive if the cannibals they ran into were to break their teeth on these scapulars.

50

S INCE MOVING TO Ranelagh, I didn't see Jacko that often any more, but one day as I was coming home from school, I ran into him at the bottom of Charlemont Street. We were headed in the same direction as far as the canal, where we'd then go our separate ways. I figured that was enough time for a bit of a laugh but not enough for Jacko to get us into trouble. I should have known better.

We'd no sooner started off together than it began to rain, so we ran for the number forty-four double-decker bus that was at the stop ahead. I said there was no point as the driver would only pull away as soon as he saw us running for it. But, strangely enough, the bus hadn't moved by the time we got to it, so we hopped on and sat downstairs at the back. There was no sign of the conductor. Obviously he was upstairs collecting fares, so Jacko reached around from his seat and dinged the bell twice for him. Two dings for go, one ding for stop.

Everybody turned and looked at us in a funny way when the bus started up; as though we shouldn't be there; as though we'd done something wrong. We had! As the bus pulled away from the stop and gathered speed, I looked out the back window and saw the conductor come tearing out of Black's shop with a packet of cigarettes in his hands. Jayzis, he hadn't been upstairs after all; he'd been in the shop buying smokes. The driver obviously didn't see him in his mirror, just kept going and gathering speed. Letting a roar out of him, the conductor took off after the bus like a greyhound. Belting down the middle of the road, cigarette packet between his teeth, peaked busman's cap clamped to his head with one hand, money bag around his neck flying from its strap behind him, the other hand holding the ticket machine that bounced at his waist, he was a sight you don't see too often on the streets of Dublin. In a panic, I hit the bell but, of course, the driver wouldn't pull up until we reached the next bus stop. When I thought about it, I was glad of that. It would give us a bit of a head start before the fuming conductor caught up on us. He was still going strong behind us, and if a horse-and-cart or something got in the way of the bus and slowed it down, we'd be snookered. The cap had blown away by this and the conductor's hair was slick with rain. His hands were pumping at his side like pistons – hands that I hoped wouldn't get anywhere near me.

When the bus stopped near the canal bridge, Jacko and me skedaddled across the road, through the gates of St Ultan's Hospital, down the corridor and out the back. The last view I had of the conductor was him doubled over, limping up to the back of the bus with his hands between his legs. I'd say the heavy ticket machine hanging around his waist was the cause of that. Although he hadn't seen it, I knew my face would give the game away if I met that conductor ever again, so from then on, even if it meant waiting in the rain an extra ten minutes for the next one, the number forty-four bus became to me like one of those occasions of sin we were learning about in school – something to be avoided at all cost.

51

THE LARK WAS a man, not a Christian Brother, and the best thing about him was that he wasn't much of a biffer. Of course, he'd biff sometimes – you couldn't be a master and not biff – but he didn't do it that often. And when he did biff, he didn't look comfortable about doing it, so somehow you felt a bit sorry for him – as long as it wasn't you that was being biffed, of course. The thing was, he never looked as though he enjoyed biffing like some of the others did. Oh, they all said they hated to have to do it but it was their painful duty. And they'd say things like, "This hurts me more than it hurts you." Did you ever hear such a load of old cobblers in your life?

Maybe the Lark felt he didn't have to be a biffer, that the stern look of him was enough, because he could look awful fierce when he took a mind to. He certainly gave the feeling that he could become a serious biffer if that's what was needed, so just watch it. His hair was cut straight across like a brush, as though the top to his head was flat. You never knew what might be going on in a head like that. One morning, though, he didn't look stern. Well, he looked stern all right, but also like he wished he was invisible. "What happened, Mr Larkin?" everyone wanted to know when they saw his chin covered with bits of newspaper that had been stuck there to stop the bleeding.

"Right," he said. "Let's get it out in the open, have a laugh, and then down to work. The razor was what did it to me. I got a new razor. An electric razor. Don't, boys, I advise you, get an electric razor when you start to shave. It's an implement of the devil, an unnatural, bloodthirsty implement of torture. I wouldn't give one to my worst enemy. Right, that's it. You know it all now." He turned to the board, shot out his cuff and got the chalk going.

High up on the wall, between the two windows, was a loud-speaker. There was one in each classroom, and they were all

connected back to Brother Devoy's office. From there he could lead
the prayers for the whole school every morning and give out important information. He'd click it on and tell about sports meetings,
maybe, or the special retreat for schoolboys that the Capuchin
monks might be holding out in Raheny. One time, after the click,
Brother Devoy told us that a musician would be in the school next
week with mouth organs that we could buy from him for so much a
week and he would teach us to play for free; and he said something
about music having the power to charm savages.

Sure enough, the man came, took the first instalment, and
handed over the shiny, silver, tissue-paper-wrapped Bandmaster
mouth organs and gave us our first lesson. After that, he came
every week for a half an hour for another lesson. But just as we
were beginning to get the hang of it, weren't the mouth organs
paid off and he never showed his face again. "The Harp That
Once" was one of the songs we tried to learn. "The Minstrel Boy"
was another. Each note on the mouth organ had a number on it,
and the man wrote the number of the note you wanted on the
blackboard. You blew into a number unless he'd put a bracket
around it. Those bracketed numbers you sucked. Blow, blow,
suck, suck, blow, suck, blow, blow, blow, blow. Mind you, with the
whole class going at it together, only that the name was on the
board over the suck and blow numbers, you wouldn't have a clue
what the song was. The Lark stayed the first morning, but after
that he would excuse himself when the mouth-organ man
showed up – so as not to be in the way of the sad music of human-
ity, he said.

Most of the time, the loudspeaker was hanging on the wall doing
nothing, and this must have seemed a waste to Brother Devoy,
because sometimes he'd switch it on and then off again without a
word coming out of it, like he was hoping the act of switching it on
would give him inspiration, but it hadn't. You'd hear the click and
then the sort of empty sound of nothing that hums out of a loudspeaker when it's not speaking. Of course, all work in the class would
stop. The Lark's chalk would stop moving, and all pens and pencils
would stop writing while everyone listened. Then you'd hear the
click of the loudspeaker going off, and the sound of nothing would

be replaced by a different sound of nothing. By now, you'd have forgotten what you were doing, and so would the Lark.

He'd say, "Now, where were we? Oh, yes." And he'd shake his
head, almost like he was angry with Brother Devoy, although that
couldn't be, could it? But sometimes, going by the look on his
face as the class would slowly get started again, I imagined that
the Lark wouldn't mind giving Brother Devoy an electric razor for
Christmas.

One of Brother Devoy's loudspeaker inspirations was the idea of
playing music while you were at your lessons. After the click got
everyone's attention, he told the whole school that an experiment
had been done in America that proved that music could make you
better at your school work. Very progressive they were in America.
Starting on Monday, he said, inspiring music would play when we
were at our lessons and turn us all into geniuses.

On Monday after the morning prayers, the whole school was on
edge, waiting, listening, anticipating. The loudspeaker hummed
its little nothing noise for a moment. Then there was the amplified
thud of a needle dropping on to the middle of a record; then the
screech as it was captured and dragged back to the start. The
record went racing off now at the wrong speed altogether until,
with a squeal like a stuck pig, it ground to a halt. When it finally
did get under way at the right speed, from the right place, "The
Blue Danube" waltz came trickling out of the loudspeaker. It was
going to take a while to get used to this strange, new, better, American way of doing lessons. Actually nobody was doing any lessons
at all. Concentration, the one thing Brother Devoy said the music
would bring – according to the experiment – was a long way off.

I'm not sure who started it. Maybe it was Gerry Jacobs. Anyway,
whoever it was, one voice started humming quietly along with the
music. Then another quiet voice joined in with made-up words.
Then somebody else took it up and improved on the words. Now
the whole class was in on it, everyone trying to outdo each other
with new lines. The Lark, who was a bit deaf anyway, was at the
blackboard with his back to us and, over the noise of the loudspeaker, couldn't hear what was going on. If he had looked
around, he would have seen a room full of giggling schoolboys

holding their sides in convulsions trying to keep from laughing out loud. Some boys had tears in their eyes and some were so near to exploding that the tears were running out of their noses on top of their copybooks as they fumbled for handkerchiefs. The whole class was singing under its breath now to the tune of "The Blue Danube", and each new line added made it harder than ever to keep a straight face.

> *It's all on your leg, gic-gic, la-la.*
> *It's two inches thick, gic-gic, la-la.*
> *It's making me sick, gic-gic, la-la.*
> *Get to the lav quick, gic-gic, la-la.*
> *It's so slick, we'll be sick, go quick. La-la.*

52

PEOPLE SAID THERE was something peculiar about Mr Bowes, but they would never elaborate when I asked them what they meant. "Oh, now," they'd say. "Just don't say you weren't warned."

"Warned about what?"

"Oh, now," they'd say again, nodding and winking at the same time. "'Nough said." And I'd be left puzzling over what they were on about.

The Boweses, Mr and Miss, brother and sister, ran a newsagent's shop on the main road. The sign over the door said they sold Newspapers and Smoker's Requisites. It didn't say that they also sold sweets, but they did. The wrapped sweets – Sailor's Chew, Honey Bees and such – were on display in open boxes on the counter; the unwrapped ones were in wide-mouthed glass jars with screw-on lids and had scoops in them to dish out the sweets into brown paper bags. Cleeve's Toffee came in a slab that was kept under the counter along with the heavy knife and hammer used to smash it into edible squares that cost a ha'penny each. I could never understand why it didn't come in separate squares to start with. Who ever heard of anyone buying a whole slab? That would probably cost a shilling – maybe more. For a penny, you got twelve Nancy Balls wrapped in a cone made from torn-up newspaper. A gobstopper that you could suck all day also cost a penny. You took it out of your mouth from time to time to make sure it was changing colour as it should: red, green, purple, orange, until – just before you swallowed it – it turned white in surrender.

On shelves behind the counter, brightly coloured cigarette packets – Gold Flake, Sweet Afton, Woodbine, Capstan – were stacked in groups separated from each other by little pyramids of matchboxes from the Friendly Match Company. For the thinking man who smoked a pipe, tobacco wrapped in foil – Honey Dew, Walnut

Plug, Erinmore, Bendigo Plug – was kept in a deep drawer under the cash register. The pipes were on display in a glass case. Pipes with bent stems and with straight stems, with big bowls and small bowls, bowls with thick walls and bowls with thin walls, bowls that were plain, carved, smooth or knobbly. There was even one pipe that you could fold up and put in your pocket if you wanted.

On hanging cards were tin lids to cover the pipe bowls to keep the ash in and the rain out; there were gadgets with little arms that opened out, each arm having a special function to do with the pipe ritual; there were pen knives for slicing the plug tobacco into smokable slivers; and there were long packets of pipe cleaners. The pipe cleaners were for pushing through the pipe to clean out the guck, but some of the women on Portobello Road used to use them as hair curlers. You'd get the glimpse under a scarf of a fuzzy pipe cleaner twisted around a damp curl when they were going to the shops, maybe, or washing the steps.

The Boweses' counter went around two sides of the little shop, and behind the counter was the door, always kept closed, leading to the living quarters beyond. The window in this door was veiled with lace curtains. I wondered what it was like behind those clean, lace curtains, but never got more than an occasional, brief glimpse, as when the door would open and close smartly to let one of the Boweses rapidly through, or to let Miss Bowes sweep some dust briskly out into the shop with the customers – where, pre-sumably, it belonged.

Now that I was delivering newspapers for them, I was in the shop twice every day. In the morning, it was mostly copies of the *Irish Press* I delivered, although there were a few *Irish Independents*; and there was one lonely *Irish Times* that went to one of the big houses on Park Drive. In the evenings, my sack was full of *Heralds*, *Mails* and *Evening Presses*.

In spite of what people said, I thought Mr Bowes was nice, always slipping me a couple of Honey Bees when Miss Bowes wasn't looking – which wasn't that often. Because if either of them was peculiar, it was Miss Bowes, in my opinion. She watched her brother like a hawk all the time, as though he would steal all the sweets if she didn't keep an eye on him. But sure, what harm would a couple of Honey Bees do? That wouldn't break them. And she watched me too; I could feel it. If I looked in her direction when I felt her gaze, her face would snap away and be looking elsewhere, but I knew I was right. You could almost see the spin marks in the air. Why did she look at me like that? Didn't she trust me either?

Behind the counter, beside the window was a kitchen chair with the back broken off, and there Miss Bowes would sit to watch the comings and goings on the street or to write the address on each paper for me before putting it in the canvas sack in order of delivery. Then, with the sack on the back carrier, I would cycle off on the paper round. Sometimes Miss Bowes was behind the counter by herself when I came back with the empty sack. Sometimes Mr Bowes was there along with her. But Mr Bowes was never there by himself. Except one time. One time, I came back from the evening round and Mr Bowes was alone. Even more surprising, he wasn't sitting beside the window on the backless chair but was out from behind the counter on the customers' side. He nodded in his usual friendly fashion and pointed to the open box of Honey Bees. "Go on. Take a few," he said. Smiling my thanks, I did so.

Mr Bowes was funny-looking. Not fat exactly but sort of . . . bulky . . . square. A block. And smooth. His skin was pale and so smooth that it looked stretched. It shone on the top of his bald head like it had been polished. His flat feet caused him to move slowly and awkwardly, like he was wearing flippers. Mr Bowes was an awkward, slow-moving, smooth block. His hands were large and smooth. His head was bald and smooth. His cheeks were close-shaved and smooth. The only hair visible on him was the grey moustache on his upper lip, and that didn't really look much like hair at all, more like a small version of a road sweeper's broom. Stiff and spiky, the moustache formed a veil from behind which his upper plate would fall down into his mouth from time to time.

"You're a good boy. A nice boy," he said, as I laid the empty sack on the counter. His teeth went click. I straightened up when I felt the warm breath on my neck. Mr Bowes's warm breath. Stepping away from him, I found himself in the dark space behind the shop door. Wedged between the door and the counter, there was no way out except toward Mr Bowes. Puzzled, I looked at the man, this smooth block of a man moving slowly in my direction. Instinct – it wasn't revulsion, not yet – caused me to step even further back into the corner from which there was no escape. In the distance the bell of Beechwood Avenue Church began to ring for the Angelus. *The angel of the Lord declared unto Mary.*

The smooth, hairless hands were on my shoulders now. They rested there for a moment, as though they were lost and were trying to decide which way to go. Then they moved down my back and began gently pulling me toward Mr Bowes's lowering face. *And she conceived of the Holy Ghost.* I didn't resist. Didn't know how to resist. Or even what it was I should be resisting. Mesmerised, I watched the spiky moustache descend in the direction of my mouth. It seemed to come very slowly and from very far away. The bristles looked tough, like nails driven through the upper lip from the inside. They were matched by smaller nails inside the nostrils. Nostrils that looked huge, like giant candle snuffers, coming down to snuff out . . . what?

Turning my face quickly away, I felt the rough tuft of moustache rake across my cheek. What was the man trying to do? My lowered eyes took in the newspapers on the counter. *Irish Independents, Irish Presses* and *Irish Timeses*. Why are they all called the Irish this and the Irish that? Aren't we in Ireland? Do they think we don't know where we are? *Be it done unto me according to thy word.* I could feel the base of my ear being nuzzled by the spiky moustache. Mr Bowes's cheek wasn't as smooth as it looked; it rasped. I stood without moving, not resisting, totally baffled, not knowing what to do.

"Georgie! Stop that! This instant!" Miss Bowes was somewhere in the background. "Do you hear me, you awful man?" Miss Bowes was angry. Screaming. "Stop it now!" Georgie? That was his name – Georgie? It sounded so silly that I wanted to laugh out loud but couldn't. The man stepped hurriedly backward.

"Ah, now, now. Don't get excited," he was saying. Although he was the one sounded excited, like he was out of breath, "I was just giving the boy a friendly hug." Then, for once moving quickly, he was around the counter and into the room at the back of the shop. I looked up from the papers on the counter in time to see the lace curtains fly up on the rapidly closing door. Miss Bowes in her hat

and coat, having just come in from the street, was on my side of the
counter, looking anxious.

"Are you all right?" she said. "You mustn't mind my brother.
He's a good man, but he has his little peculiarities, his little weak-
nesses. You won't say anything, sure you won't? There's a good
lad."

She looked anxiously at me as she spoke. I was puzzled; she
looked so scared. I wondered what she was afraid of. She's not
afraid of me, is she? She spoke again. "You won't, sure you won't?
Say anything?" Mind in turmoil and mouth dry, I just looked at
her, stupefied. I tried to answer, but my mouth was too parched to
make the words. A shake of the head. No, I wouldn't say anything.
In the silence between us, the Angelus bell clanged on.

Suddenly the corner I was in was so claustrophobic that I
couldn't bear it any longer. Lurching forward, I spun around the
door as Miss Bowes spoke again. "You're a good boy, so you are. A
nice boy." Then, most unlike her, she thrust a handful of Honey
Bees in my direction, but I didn't stop for them. I was on the move
and couldn't stop now even if I'd wanted to. My feet had decided
to take me home. *And the word was made flesh. And dwelt amongst us.*

53

"**D**O YOU WANT to go up and see him?" Uncle Bill asked. I hesitated, not sure how to answer that question. "Go on," he said. "He was always very fond of you, you know." He gave a smile that was meant to be encouraging but wasn't much of a smile at all, just a pressing together of the lips for an instant and then it was gone. Slowly, I went up the stairs in my granda's house. From the landing, I looked down over the banisters and saw that the hall below was empty. Nobody would know whether I went into the bedroom or not, but I was drawn toward it anyway. The fingers of my left hand walked along the banister rail and didn't stop until I was outside the door. Taking a deep breath, I knocked. As soon as my knuckles hit the white-painted wood, I wanted to bite the hand off. Stuffing it deep into the pocket of my trousers, I took another deep breath. Who did I suppose was going to answer the knock? Or, more to the point, what would I have done if my granda had said, "Come in"? My granda who was dead.

I creaked open the door. Now I knew what people meant when they said their hearts were in their mouths, because that's what it felt like. Or, if it wasn't in my mouth, it was as close as could be, fluttering like a scared thing high up in my chest. Gulping it down, I prepared for my first look at a dead person.

The bedroom was dim because the blind was pulled down. That's what you did when somebody was dead, pulled down the blinds; a mark of respect, they said it was. But a bit of the grey daylight leaked disrespectfully into the room around the blind's buckled edges, and the frills along the bottom of it rippled thoughtlessly in the breeze from the slightly open window. I forced myself to look toward the bed where my granda lay. Morris had said dead people were easy. "Look like they're sleeping is all. Nothing to be feared of," he said. Morris was wrong. My granda didn't look like he was sleeping. He looked dead. More, he looked like he was made of wax and had never been alive. Whatever that was, there on the bed, it had nothing to do with my granda. The hands had been folded across the chest, and the fingers were linked around a string of rosary beads. I had never seen beads anywhere near my granda. A pipe now, that would have been more in keeping. His little finger stuck up a bit, as though waiting for the pipe stem to be slid in under it.

As I swung the door closed behind me, something rattled. It was my granda's lighthouse-keeper's jacket swinging on its hanger on the back of the door. Brass buttons flashed as though the little lighthouse on each button was sending out a ray to guide me safely to the bedside. Say a wee prayer, I'd been told, for the repose of your granda's soul. I couldn't think of any prayers, only something I'd heard that morning. According to the wireless, a man in England had run a mile in under four minutes. Nobody had ever run that fast before; it was a record. The fact that anybody would want to would have amused my granda, who'd have said something like, "Sounds like a bit of a greyhound to me. Does he sleep in a kennel and eat dog biscuits, do y'think? And go to the lav in the bushes."

I reached out and touched the hands that looked like they were made of putty. Like a marble statue dead people were said to be. But a statue would get warm if you held it long enough. No amount of heat would warm those hands. They would take every bit of heat out of your body, those hands would, and come back looking for more.

The thing was, my granda shouldn't have died at all, they said. If only he'd stayed where he was in the hospital, they said. If he hadn't taken the wrong turning, he'd be with us yet, they said. What he'd done was get up out of the hospital bed when no one was looking, slip his clothes on over his pyjamas, and set out from the centre of the city to walk home because he didn't have his bike or his bus fare. All he had on him when they found him was a box of matches. Nobody could understand how he'd missed the turn for Collins Avenue. A man who'd been criss-crossing the city of Dublin on his bike for years and knew it like the back of his hand;

how could he have gone by the end of the road that would have taken him to his home in Donnycarney? Halfway to Howth he was when they found him, lying in the gutter with his hip broken where he'd slipped off the footpath. And only he missed the turn, they said, he'd have been safe in his own house ages before, so he would. They sent him home from the hospital soon after, and he just faded away to nothing there in the bed. All said it was because his mind must have been wandering that he hadn't been able to find his way to Donnycarney that day. Sure, couldn't he have found the place in the dark and him blindfolded?

I thought so, too; that's why I knew they were the ones on the wrong track, not my granda. He hadn't taken the wrong road. He hadn't been heading for Donnycarney at all. If they found him on the road to Howth, it could only be because he was heading for Howth. The box of matches in his pocket was the giveaway. He'd been on his way out to the Baily Lighthouse in Howth to light the lamp to make sure nobody'd be lost at sea that night.

Would he meet Robin Hood in heaven? Robin Hood would like my granda, who would fit in very well and be the merriest of the Merry Men, although there probably wouldn't be much call for a lighthouse in Sherwood Forest.

While the tea and stout and whiskey and sandwiches were keeping everybody occupied in the kitchen, I went out the back to the little shed that had been my granda's workshop. The shop-coat he used to wear in the workshop was hanging on a nail, smelling smoky, like he had just taken it off after having had the pipe going. There was a bulge in the pocket that was the tobacco pouch with a square of plug tobacco in it. The penknife wasn't there, nor was the pipe. The pouch, the plug, the penknife, the pipe: the four Ps disbanded for ever. Propped against the wall was his bike that must be nearly as old as him, because I had never seen him with any other. Nor was it black like everybody else's. It was dark green, painted that colour by my granda himself, who kept it spick and span at all times. The wheel rims had a thin coating of Vaseline to keep the rust at bay, and the hubs had little leather straps hanging loosely around them to spin away the dust. The back carrier used to open up into a seat that I would sit in to get taken for a ride when I was little. I pulled on it now and it opened as easy as pie: it had been kept oiled and ready for action all these years.

Many's the time I had watched as the bike got its oil rations. The big chain that made the whole thing go and the little chain that went into the hub of the back wheel for the three speed, and the pedals and the axles and brake rods and every other moving part had been given its sup of oil every week. Climbing up on the work-bench, I took down the oilcan and went over the bike with it because I knew nobody else would think to do it this weekend.

The next morning, after the mass for the dead where the angels were instructed to lead him into paradise, my granda's coffin was carried out of the chapel by handles that hung like big door knockers from the sides – knockers you could bang on for ever without getting an answer. The coffin was slid into the back of the hearse, which led the way slowly down the drive and out into the traffic. It drove to his house, still with its window blinds down, and stopped for a few moments. All the houses on the street had the blinds down. A sign of respect for the dear departed. Was this why the hearse had stopped, so Granda could see how respected he was? I looked up at the window of the room where the wax dummy of him had been the day before. The handle of the pulled-down blind was sticking out the bottom of the open window, its tassels waving goodbye.

As we turned down Collins Avenue, a guard got off his bike, stood to attention and saluted. Other guards we passed did the same, and people all along the route were stopping on the foot-path and blessing themselves. I was very proud of my granda that day; who would have thought he'd been so well known? Even the traffic stopped to let us go through red lights.

The sea was out the right-hand window now, and I thought I recognised the spot. "Where are we going, Dad?" I asked. My dad was holding my mam's gloved hand in his lap and looking out at the water, a bit glassy-eyed.

"What?" he said, like he hadn't heard, but then he answered the question. "Howth," he said. "The graveyard is halfway up the Hill of Howth. A very healthy graveyard it is, too – because it's so near the sea." His lips gave a little bit of a twitch like he was going to smile, but he didn't. He just gave the gloved hand in his lap a squeeze.

Howth. So, my granda would get there after all. The last place in the world he'd been trying to get to. Now he'd be able to keep an eye on all the lighthouses around Dublin Bay. I hoped they'd remembered to put the matches back in his pocket. And I was glad I'd oiled the bike for him, because my granda would be lost in heaven without it. On the last day, when Jacko's dad's bike rose from the canal all rusted and ruined, and all the other bockety bikes of the world ascended and were chained to the gates of heaven, wouldn't his be the best one there and the envy of all.

My granda was pulled backward from the hearse and carried by the men on the last bit of his last journey to his last resting place. Among the stone angels and crosses and tombstones and faded wreaths, the coffin swayed and lumbered toward the hole in the ground like some awkward, reluctant animal. Piled to one side, fresh, brown, gluey earth spilled over the grass and attached itself to shoes to be carried away from this place. A memento.

All eyes seemed to be wet and glistening now: my mam's, my dad's, my grandma's, my Uncle Bill's, everyone's. But sure, hadn't the priest said Granda was in God's presence now in heaven? Why was everyone crying if he was better off than he'd ever been before? Were they all jealous or what?

The grave men slid Granda down into the hole on two ropes, and when they pulled the ropes up again, he was gone. Looping the coffin-less ropes over their hands and down under their elbows, they coiled them like cowboy's lassos. The priest said some words in Latin – a dead language for a dead granda – and sprinkled the grave with holy water from a little brush like the one beside the fireplace at home.

Giving up on the prayers, the priest stepped back, and the grave men came from behind with their shovels and threw a cascade of dirt and stones down into the hole, where it smashed, sharp and merciless, against the coffin. At that unexpected and brutal sound, I suddenly felt all choked up, unable to breathe, like I was expanding and contracting at the same time. Keeping the wail that wanted to escape bottled up inside, I tried to ease my throat by swallowing, but every swallow felt as though a hacksaw blade inside was rasping against my Adam's apple.

The earth raining down on Granda sounded like the rattle of my knuckles on the bedroom door yesterday. Like the earth was knocking to get into the coffin beside him and make him one with it. The lump in my throat grew big as a football, and stinging tears ran down my face and dripped from my chin. Nothing had prepared me for the sledgehammer blow of grief that had just smacked into me. In a way I couldn't understand, I knew I was crying for more than my dead granda. I was crying for me. And for my mam and dad. And for all the living and the dead and the not-yet born. For a world of never-ending funerals. Not trying to hide the tears any longer, I stood, wet face open now to the chill wind blowing in off Dublin Bay and up the side of the Hill of Howth to search among the gravestones and finger us all.

54

I WAS BEGINNING TO think that maybe there *was* something in what Bermo's mam had said that day about the first-born being a bit bockety. The dreams I was having these days were certainly bockety. I used to have one when I was younger, about lassoing Jenny Hooper on the canal bank and making her take her clothes off. How she was supposed to get them off while she had a rope round her, I didn't know. But she did it. In my dream, there she stood in front of me, all two-foot-nine of her, peeled off down to her liberty bodice. But that wasn't a patch on the dreams I was having now – and I seemed to be turning into a monster.

Big pimples were bursting through my chin, and hair was beginning to grow between my legs. Was I turning into a werewolf? But bad as these things were, there was something far worse that seemed to afflict me only when I was in bed. Some mornings, I'd wake with my mickey like a poker. What was the matter with me at all? There wasn't anybody I could talk to about it, I was that ashamed. My dad? Jayzis! I imagined the scene.

"The thing is, Dad, me mickey . . . well, in the mornin's, it doesn't be hangin' down like a normal mickey. It does be standin' up stiff an' about a hundred times bigger than it usually is." I was sure to be hauled off to the doctor; and by then it would have shrunk back to normal size again, and they wouldn't believe me. Oh God oh God oh God oh God! Is there something terribly wrong with me? Have I some terrible stiffening disease that might spread maybe to the rest of me? I'd heard of hardening of the arteries. Perhaps that's what it was. And the fear that if I tripped getting out of bed, I'd fall on it and break it off. Or pole-vault out the window.

But then, by accident, I found a solution. While wrestling with it one morning, didn't I find out how to make it relax and lie down? When force hadn't worked, I'd switched to the gentle touch, the coaxing, caressing stroke. Then, without warning, my hand accelerated, as though it had a mind of its own. Now it was going as though it was shaking a bottle of lemonade to make it fizz. Then I let out a gasp of surprise and the next thing, wasn't wetness that I couldn't control spurting out between my fingers. Jayzis! Was I bleeding to death? Trying to hold myself from leaking all over the bed, with my right hand, I undid the pyjama cord with my left and lifted the covers. The hand not holding up the bedclothes was squeezed in a fist over the spurting wound. Jesus Christ! I've broken the thing right off, that's what I've done. But for all that my heart was pounding with panic, there was an extraordinary relaxed sweetness flowing through me at the same time. And my mind was clear as anything. Maybe it wasn't the end of the world. Maybe they could sew it back on. I'd heard of a man down the country whose finger had been bitten off by a dog and, after they'd shot the dog, sewn back on again.

When I finally unclenched the fist and looked, I found no wound. Where the stiffness had been, there was only the normal, soft, pink thing I was used to. The few downy hairs were coated with a milky fluid and my fingers were sticky, but obviously no surgery was called for. Everything was all right so.

Mind you, there was still the mystery of where the hardness had come from. And where had it gone to now? Raising the blanket, I looked again at the relaxed little cluster. Sure that yoke was only for peeing with. That other big thing was after something else. Like there was a submarine inside that had sent up its periscope to look for . . . what?

Well, whatever strange disease I had, I decided I wasn't going to die from it anyway, because however often it happened, I always recovered. In fact, there were times I didn't even get involved. It just kind of went off by itself when I was asleep. I'd wake up and my pyjamas would be stiff in the front like they sometimes got if they were hung on the line in winter.

Another thing, the strangest thing, sometimes I found myself looking at girls in the street. Sneakily, of course. It wouldn't do to let them catch me looking, that'd be the last straw, but for some reason I couldn't keep my eyes off them. I tried to talk sense to myself, but I wouldn't listen. My eyes wouldn't do what they were told, no more than my thoughts would. And I couldn't make head nor tail of the thoughts. Maybe it was the opportunity I had to view girls in the quiet emptiness of the mornings that brought it on. Now that I was delivering papers again – for Keighron's this time – I was out in the streets early and would see them, all fresh and crisp and clean, on their way to school. Swaying down the footpath or swishing by on their bikes or, better still, getting *on* their bikes, they made my heart drop into my stomach. How I wished they would – but girls didn't – throw their legs over the saddle the way boys did. Because girl's bikes had no crossbars, they just straddled the bike and then sat back with their gymslips tucked under them and off they went, long legs pumping. Where had all these girls come from all of a sudden? I'd never noticed them before, and now the streets seemed to be flooded with them.

There was one who lived on Beechwood Avenue. The first time I saw her, I ran into the back of a parked car. It was such a whack that I bent the bike's crossbar, like I'd done to my dad's a long time ago. Of course, the girl looked over when she heard the bang, so I had to pretend I'd done it on purpose; that bent crossbars were all the rage. Whistling, I admired my handiwork studiously from various angles, trying to look very satisfied with what I'd accomplished. When I looked again, the girl was gone.

After that, I always made sure I happened to be accidentally passing her house in the morning when she came out her gate – even if it took a couple of trips around the block to bring it off. From her green uniform, I could tell that she went to Muckross College on Marlborough Road. Although it was against everything I believed in, I almost felt I wanted to speak to her. But whenever her face turned toward me, instead of opening my gob, I turned away and cycled on, aloof as anything. Halfway up the road, I'd convince myself not to be so stupid; she was only a girl. But by the time I'd have turned around and cycled back, she'd be with her friends or on the bus and gone. I couldn't understand why my heart would be going like the clappers and why I felt so muddled. I gave out yards to myself for allowing the day to be spoiled before it had even begun. Because it *was* spoiled. For the rest of the morning now, I'd be calling myself all sorts of an eejit for not opening my mouth. And then I'd waste the afternoon planning what I'd say to her tomorrow morning.

So now it seemed I had girls to contend with as well as wet dreams; where would it all end? The thought that there might be a connection between the two was just too confusing altogether. At least until the school retreat given in Harrington Street Chapel, that is. Then things began to fall dimly into place. If I was bockety, I wasn't the only one.

55

"**M**Y DEAR LITTLE brothers in Christ," intoned the priest from the pulpit. "You are reaching the age when you will soon be making your confirmation. You are well on the way to being young men, so you are. But you will always be children of God, and you must never forget that you have but one soul to save. One God to love and serve. One eternity to prepare for. Death will come soon. Judgement will follow, and then, my dear little boys – heaven or hell for ever! Mother of Perpetual Succour, pray for us."

That was the usual sort of stuff, and nobody, except maybe the Dalton brothers, got too excited by it. But when the priest began talking in a way that made it seem as though he was suffering from morning stiffness himself, or at least knew somebody who was, suddenly everyone was all attention.

"You must respect your bodies. Your body is God's temple. You must be vigilant against impure thoughts. Which of you would invite a guest to your home having purposely made the place uninhabitable? Well, that is what you do to the temple of the Lord when you defile and pollute your bodies with your own impure touches." His voice rose and his fist came down with a clatter on the pulpit rail. "I'm talking about clutching at yourselves under the blankets in the morning, so I am. Get up out of it at once. Say a prayer to Almighty God and His Holy Mother for the strength, and get up from out of that warm occasion of sin. For the devil finds work for idle hands, and to linger is to do the devil's work. Because the devil watches and encourages you in your weakness. Oh, yes, he does. 'Go on,' he says. 'What harm?' he says. 'Sure, isn't it nice?' he says. And you maybe going to receive holy communion that morning. Well, my dear little brothers in Christ, let me tell you that you cannot receive the sacrament with that sin on your soul. That would be to take Almighty God into a defiled temple, a charnel house, and that would be a mortal sin. If you were to die then with that sin on your immortal soul, you would go straight to hell, so you would. Down there in that pit with the devil and his minions, you would burn for all eternity, and all because you wouldn't get out of bed in the morning. In the name of the Father, and of the Son, and of the Holy Ghost."

There was dead quiet in the chapel. A chapel is always quiet, of course, but this was a weighty quiet, a meaningful quiet – a gleefully shocked silence, in fact. In those few moments, every scholar in the place recognised his kinship with every other scholar. Polluters to a boy. Nobody admitted doing it himself, of course, but everyone was perfectly willing to believe that everyone else was guilty of it. The ultimate derogatory call became, "Don't mind yer man. He's only a wanker." "The pot," as my mam would have had it in one of her sayings, "calling the kettle black".

But none of this helped the girl problem much. All right, I wasn't a monster. Or, at least, not the only monster. And the book I read wasn't much better. Knowing it was hormones or something didn't help the shame nor make it easier to talk to girls. It just tied the two of them together, making it twice as bad. What would the girl in the Muckross uniform think if she knew the work I was doing with the devil's idle hands?

Every morning for weeks, I watched for her on Beechwood Avenue. Every morning for weeks, I meant to talk to her. Every morning for weeks, I cycled past her with my nose in the air. But then one morning, I didn't. Or at least, I did, but she called out a good morning to me. And she knew my name! Before I knew what I was doing, I'd jammed on the brakes; front one first, unfortunately. I knew better than to do that because of what could happen. And it did. The back wheel tried to change places with the front wheel. The newspapers that were on the back carrier flew over my head and I followed headfirst after them, landing with such a thump that I was stunned for a moment. Sparkles went off in front of my eyes, and, only it was daylight, I'd have thought they were stars. *Féach, réaltaí sa spéir.*

There I was, sitting in the middle of all the news from all around the world, but none of it came close in importance to the nearness of this girl who was standing looking down on me, real haughty with her hand on her hip. Inches away, the short, pleated, school uniform danced on her thigh with the jiggling of her dimpled knee. Mesmerised, not even aware of the indignity of my position, I sat, Adam's apple moving up and down dryly. I wished I could speak. Or swallow. Or anything.

"Do you not recognise me?" she said.

What did she mean, recognise her? Of course, I recognised her. Hadn't I seen her nearly every morning for the past two months? How could I not recognise her? I looked at her again, paying more attention. There was a superior air about her, a smug air, as though she knew something I didn't. And she reminded me of somebody. Who was it? She looked a bit like . . . I had a flash of a bleached golliwog in a holy communion dress. It couldn't be. Jayzis, it was.

Assumpta Jordan! Talk about bockety.

SOME OTHER READING

from

Brandon is a leading publisher of new fiction and non-fiction for an international readership. For a catalogue of new and forthcoming books, please write to
Brandon/Mount Eagle, Unit 3 Olympia Trading Estate, Coburg Road, Wood Green, London N22 6TZ, England; or Brandon/Mount Eagle, Cooleen, Dingle, Co. Kerry, Ireland. For a full listing of all our books in print, please go to

www.brandonbooks.com

LILY O'CONNOR
Can Lily O'Shea Come Out to Play?

A bestseller in Ireland and Australia, a fascinating story of growing up Protestant in Dublin.

"Anyone with half an interest in times gone by will enjoy this well-written anecdotal book."
Irish Criticism

"A vibrant recollection of childhood, this — honest, warm and often moving." *Examiner*

ISBN 0 86322 267 6; paperback

Dreams of Hope

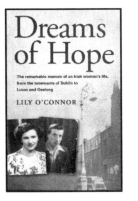

A sparkling memoir with the appeal of *Don't Wake Me at Doyles* and *Angela's Ashes*; a sequel to her successful first book, *Can Lily O'Shea Come Out to Play?*, this is a remarkable personal account of the emigrant lives of one Irish couple amongst the hundreds upon thousands forced to emigrate from Dublin in the 1950s.

ISBN 0 86322 358 3; paperback original

MAY O'BRIEN
Clouds on My Windows

May O'Brien was fifteen in 1947 when she started to work in Liberty Hall, headquarters if the Irish Transport and General Workers' Union.

"This is a wonderful book... May O'Brien says in her afterword that this is an ordinary book about Dublin life in the 40s. Maybe it is. But it's a story about an extraordinary woman, in any time."
Irish Independent

ISBN 086322 335 4; *paperback original*

ROSEMARY CONRY
Flowers of the Fairest

"Has the ring of authenticity. This is a book to be recommended. . . Surprisingly, the story is told with much humour." *Irish Independent*

"A fascinating first-hand account of one child's experience of TB in the 1940s. It is full of interesting details of the little everyday routines of life on a veranda, with all its pain and its fun. . . A lovely book that gives us a fascinating insight into a world that thankfully we will never know."
Books Ireland

ISBN 0 86322 303 6; *paperback*

THE BESTSELLING MEMOIRS OF ALICE TAYLOR

To School Through the Fields

"One of the most richly evocative and moving portraits of childhood [ever] written…A journey every reader will treasure and will want to read over and over again." *Boston Herald*

ISBN 0 86322 099 1; *paperback*

Quench the Lamp

"Infused with wit and lyricism, the story centers on the 1950s when the author and her friends were budding teenagers. Taylor describes the past vividly and without complaint." *Publishers Weekly*

ISBN 0 86322 112 2; *paperback*

The Village

"What makes the story unique is Taylor's disarming style; she… has a knack for finding the universal truth in daily details." *Los Angeles Times*

ISBN 0 86322 142 4; *paperback*

Country Days

"Like Cupid, the author has an unerring aim for the heartstrings; however she can also transform the mundane into the magical." *The Irish Times*

ISBN 0 86322 168 8; *paperback*

THE BESTSELLING NOVELS OF ALICE TAYLOR

The Woman of the House

"What shines through in *The Woman of the House* is Alice Taylor's love of the Irish countryside and village life of over 40 years ago, its changing seasons and colours, its rhythm and pace." *Irish Independent*

ISBN 0 86322 249 8; paperback

Across the River

"Alice Taylor is an outstanding storyteller. Like a true seanchaí, she uses detail to signal twists in the plot or trouble ahead. It is tightly plotted fiction, an old-fashioned page-turner." *The Irish Times*

ISBN 0 86322 285 4; paperback

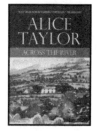

House of Memories

"*House of Memories* shows her in her prime as a novelist." *Irish Independent*

"It is Alice Taylor's strength to make the natural everyday world come alive in clear fresh prose. In this book, as in her memoirs, she does so beautifully." *The Irish Book Review*

ISBN 0 86322 352 4; paperback

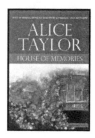